KNIFEMAKING

A COMPLETE GUIDE TO CRAFTING KNIVES, HANDLES & SHEATHS

Bo Bergman

Editors: Holly Boswell and Laura Dover Doran
Art Director and Production: Charlie Covington
Transtation: Edith M. Matteson

Library of Congress Cataloging-in-Publication Data
Bergman, Bo.
    [Knivar. English]
    Knifemaking : a complete guide to crafting knives, handles &
sheaths / Bo Bergman.
    p.   cm.
    ISBN 1-887374-37-X
    1. Metal-work. 2. Knives. I. Bergman, Bo. Knivar på mitt sätt.
English. II. Title.
TT213.B43 1997
621.9'32--DC21   97-23536
                                            CIP

10 9 8 7 6 5 4

Published by Lark Books, a division of
Sterling Publishing Co., Inc.
387 Park Avenue South, New York, N.Y. 10016

Originally published as Bo Bergman, *Knivar* and *Knivar På Mitt Sätt*,
ICA Bokförlag, 1988, 1991

English translation © 1997, Lark Books

Distributed in Canada by Sterling Publishing,
c/o Canadian Manda Group, One Atlantic Ave., Suite 105
Toronto, Ontario, Canada M6K 3E7

Distributed in the U.K. by Guild of Master Craftsman Publications Ltd., Castle Place, 166
High Street, Lewes, East Sussex, England BN7 1XU
Tel: (+ 44) 1273 477374, Fax: (+ 44) 1273 478606
Email: pubs@thegmcgroup.com, Web: www.gmcpublications.com

Distributed in Australia by Capricorn Link (Australia) Pty Ltd.
P.O. Box 704, Windsor, NSW 2756 Australia

If you have questions or comments about this book, please contact:
Lark Books
67 Broadway
Asheville, NC 28801
(828) 253-0467

Printed in Hong Kong

ISBN 1-887374-37-X

CONTENTS

FOREWORD

When I began writing and compiling this book, I was apprehensive and slightly fearful, because there was a scarcity of written material on the subject. When I asked why this scarcity existed, I was unable to get an answer. In almost every other type of handicraft, instructive and up-to-date information is available; but not in knifemaking.

Thus, I felt that I was breaking the ice for the first time when I began to fill these pages. I started to wonder if knifemakers belonged to a special guild, the activities of which nobody was allowed to mention. By giving away "secrets," would I undermine the foundation for those of us who work at this fascinating occupation? Would I be taking the bread from the mouths of handicraft workers who earn their living making knives? I don't think so. It is impossible, I think, to achieve the craftsmanship of professional knifemakers with this book and a simple wave of the wand. It takes years of practice (long after this book had been laid aside) to reach the level of the knifemaking professional. So I continued to write.

I then asked myself: What qualifications and experience do I have to share with people who want to become knifemakers? Several years of attempts and failures have resulted in a few hundred knives that meet my approval. While that may not sound very impressive, I think it is useful to learn how it all began and how I solved problems along the way.

Knives have interested me since I was a little guy. My grandfather was a carpenter, and he put the first knife in my hand and taught me the basics. Over the years, I bought knives now and then, always thinking that I had found my ideal knife. But I was never happy long. There was always something missing. The secret and mystical quality that is built into knives spoke to me and I dreamed of having the perfect knife as my companion. So I would make another trip to the store and continue searching through knife catalogs and hunting publications for the ideal knife. Finally, I grew tired, put all the knives away in storage, and did not shop for knives for several years.

Then one day I needed a knife. I went out to the storeroom and came back with a rusty old Mora knife with a wooden handle. It struck me how small the handle felt in my hand. It simply disappeared into my tight clutch. I went out and got other knives and held each of them in my hand. They were all the same! None of them had a good grip.

Then I had the idea of breaking the wooden handle of the Mora knife into pieces to attempt to make a thicker handle that fit my hand. I went out into the woods, found a piece of juniper shrub that looked as if it would work, then returned home to attach my new piece of wood to the blade.

I had never seen a knife from the inside before; when I broke open the handle, I saw that sections of it had been drilled with drill bits of various thicknesses. There was a ring-shaped cap at the end of the handle that held the whole knife together. I then began to attach my new juniper handle. After a great deal of fiddling, it began to resemble a knife. Although my newly made knife fell apart almost at once, it was the first knife I had ever owned that had a handle large enough for a man's hand.

From that point on, my knifemaking education progressed quickly. In order to obtain blades, I purchased ten new Mora knives and broke the handles apart with a screwdriver. Slowly, very slowly, the knives got a little better with each attempt. Finally I made a knife that both fit my hand and did not fall apart. My appetite was whetted.

Since there was nobody I could ask for advice, nor any book or booklet to learn from, I had to use the trial-and-error method to learn knifemaking. Each new difficulty that popped up had to be solved, and, with each solution, I learned something. I would have given a fortune for some words of wisdom along the way. I gave up several times; but, after a few days, my will would always return. Some new solution appeared and I had to try it. After a year's persistence, I even sent a few knives to a competition. Of course, my knives did not even place in the competition, but at least I had participated. Each new knife taught me a new lesson, which is true even of the knives I make today.

Much later, I found a small description of knifemaking in a newspaper article. For the first time, I could compare what I had learned with the technique of experienced knifemakers. To my amazement, I was on the right track. That was an unbelievably happy day.

I realize that I do not have anything to teach professional knifemakers. It is very likely that they will consider my advice and solutions elementary and perhaps amateurish. In the second half of this book, however, you will find some advanced projects that utilize my technique.

This book is written primarily for those who begin with little or no experience and who aren't familiar with carpentry and its various tools. This book is also for all those who have no one to ask for help and who dream of the knife becoming their lifetime companion and helper.

My intention is to help enthusiastic beginners avoid a number of the difficulties and pitfalls that I have experienced. I will attempt to describe each phase of the work process in detail and to answer all the questions that continually come up. Those who already have some experience may object to some of my solutions. They are free to do so. There are many methods in knifemaking, and some of them are probably better and quicker than mine. But I know that my methods work and they result in knives that are both strong and useful. I have tried out every new solution before I dared to continue.

So let go of your old knives, bring your tools down from the attic, and allow your imagination to take over. With a little time and patience, you will soon hold your dream knife in your hand.

Good luck!

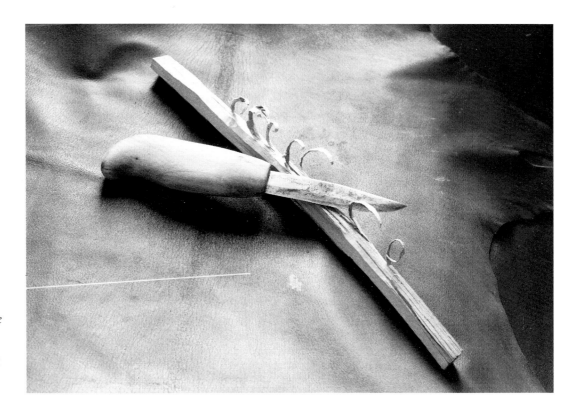

My first knife. The handle is made from juniper wood and the blade is taken from an old Mora knife. The handle split, but the knife could still be used.

MATERIALS AND TOOLS

Until a few years ago, traditional knifemaking was dying out. This was especially true of *forging*, or the practice of forming blades by heating and hammering metal. It is gratifying to notice that a growing interest in the field has begun to put life back into long-forgotten knifemaking implements and tools, and that the forges have been fired again. This newly awakened interest in knives has spurred black-smiths to return to the craft and, in turn, encouraged new knifemakers. Today, a relatively large number of excellent knifemakers create first-class, hand-forged knife blades.

THE EVER-IMPORTANT KNIFE BLADE

The knife blade is the part of the knife that you should plan to spend the most money on. The shape of the knife handle and the suitability of the sheath are also important, but the blade makes the knife into probably the most versatile and important hand tool a person can have. Even if it hurts to spend so much money at first, you will eventually get every penny back in the form of increased strength, durability, and sharpness. A knife with a good blade will come to be a true friend for life.

Any cheap steel can be sharpened, but you will soon discover that it is a waste of time. There will be endless trips to the hone, sometimes several times during the same job. On the other hand, it is a good idea to purchase some cheap blades for your first knives to practice on. Then, if something goes wrong, it won't be such a hard blow.

BLADE QUALITY

How can you determine the quality of the blade you buy? Most importantly, blades should be able to withstand common stresses without becoming damaged.

First, look at the back of the knife from directly above. A factory-made blade is often the same thick-ness from the hilt to the tip. A fine, hand-forged blade is always thickest at the point at which it goes into the handle, up to about 5 to 6 mm (about ¼ inch), then gets narrower toward the tip. (For this reason, a hand-forged blade is visibly stronger, since the stress is greatest at the point at which it enters the handle.) Rotate the blade and look at the edge from as low an angle as possible. It should be as straight as an arrow!

Otherwise, I must admit that it is hard to deter-mine at a glance whether a blade is good or not. A layman is always at a disadvantage in this respect. The blade won't reveal its true nature until it sits in the finished knife and you begin to use it.

You can find out more about the blade by testing it in all imaginable ways, then forming an opinion. Put it against the grindstone and feel how the stone "sucks in" the blade, or if you don't have a grind-stone, try an artificially made hone (for example, a diamond hone) to determine how the blade works. (A hone is a device, often a stone, used for sharpening a knife.) Check to see if the edge becomes rough or breaks easily.

By grinding the blade at various angles along the edge, it is possible to achieve a high-performance knife with acceptable sharpness and durability. Certainly versatility is limited when you do this, but you can always use the knife for something. Don't stare yourself blind trying to figure out what kind of steel is in the blade, and whether it is good or bad. What matters instead is 1) to have a good hone, 2) to be able to hone correctly, 3) to use the knife properly, and 4) to place the proper honing angle on the blade. (See page 79 for more on honing.) Also, you can be fairly certain that a blade made by a reputable manu-facturer is a quality blade.

In the old days, a good knifesmith was a person of great importance, especially for all the people who struggled in our vast backwoods for their daily bread. To drop or, in some other manner, lose your knife was a catastrophe. For ancient people, the knife was the most important tool. It was useful in times of distress. A rake could be made or repaired with it. It could shape a hasp for outhouse doors and cut birch and spruce twigs. It could make handles for other sharp-edged tools, repair broken sheaths, or cut out sole leather to make shoes. In survival hunting, it was used to butcher game and to skin all sorts of fur.

At one time, knife blades could be purchased from travelling knife-blade peddlers. But mainly it was the local blacksmith (since he also hunted) who understood all the necessary qualities of a good knife. Otherwise, knives were purchased at a chance encounter with a wandering smith or peddler, and the buyer had to be satisfied with whatever quality was available.

Today steel manufacturers supply us with steel of high and consistent quality by using material analysis and strict hardening procedures. Nonetheless, the large selection of blades today is more a source of confusion than an advantage.

In general, blades made with two types of steel are available: carbonized blades and rust-resistant blades.

CARBONIZED STEEL BLADES AND LAMINATED BLADES

Some blades are made completely of carbonized steel. *Carbonized steel blades* have an undeserved bad reputation for rusting. You will find a large selection of carbonized blades in many different grades of steel, but each manufacturer has a different idea of which type of blade is best.

In contrast to pure carbonized blades, *laminated blades* are composed of two different materials. The internal blade is made of a thin sheet of edge steel, or hard steel, that has been hardened twice to approximately 58 Rockwell (Rc). The sides of the blade are then covered with sheets of soft iron, and the entire piece is forged into one unit. The edge steel is very hard and has a high carbon content, and the soft iron sides protect the hard center steel; thus, the knife blade is not fragile, but has high durability. This process dates back to the Viking blacksmiths, a tradition that is thousands of years old.

The most expensive and finest blades are *hand-forged* or *hand-laminated* blades. The art of making this type of blade almost died out in Sweden. As far as I know, there are only a few young smiths that know this art and who sell blades of this sort today, though I'm sure there's an additional handful of older smiths who have mastered this difficult art.

Hand-forging takes great skill. Making a hand-forged masterpiece requires experience, proficiency, and keen eyes. Consequently, a hand-forged blade is quite expensive. In the most important phase of making these blades, *hardening*, the layered steel has to be hardened to exactly the right hardness. The edge will break apart if it gets too hard and will flatten or bend if it is even slightly too soft.

Carbonized steel blades are all easy to grind and hone and get very sharp. Another common feature is that they are sensitive to water and moisture. And as I said before, their potential to rust is exaggerated. If you dry off the blade after each use, then there won't be any danger of rusting. Use whatever you find around you—a dry tuft of grass, a handful of moss, or simply the leg of your pant—then put a little oil or grease on the blade when you get home. I have seen 20- to 30-year-old Mora knives that have been used frequently, but that have no rust.

In contrast to hand-forged blades, *lamell blades* are commercially made. Lamell blades from Frost's knife factory in Mora, Sweden, are now world-famous. Each and every one of us has probably had a Mora knife in our hands at some time or another. I will be careful not to praise the well-known Mora blades too much, since a Mora knife blade with a curly grained wood handle finished last in a native arts test. But the Mora blade does well in competition with other blades, regardless of the price category. Master knife-maker Sveneric Loodh has long used carbonized steel blades from Frost's knife factory in Mora in some of his knives. And he knows exactly what he's doing!

Excellent lamell blades are also made in Norway, by Brusletto and Helle, among others. I use Mora's short, narrow-tipped laminated woodworking blades for all my carpentry work.

Ultimately, whether you choose a pure carbonized steel blade or a laminated one will depend on your own taste, your wallet, and whatever you are able to find in your own neck of the woods. Both are excellent for all kinds of woodworking. Both are very versatile. It's impossible to measure which one stays sharp longer. Today, there is no objective standard by which to measure all types of blades. In addition, two blades from exactly the same manufacturer can be different. So do some experimenting and form your own opinion.

RUST-RESISTANT BLADES

The other group of steel knife blades is *rust-resistant blades*. Although the availability of rust-resistant blades is still very limited in comparison to carbonized steel, the increased demand will undoubtedly force a larger selection. One explanation for this lack of availability may be the thousand-year-old tradition of using carbonized steel and laminated steel blades. This is not easy to ignore, even though there are many advantages to using rust-resistant blades today.

Another explanation for the lack of use of rust-resistant blades may be their reputation for being impossible, or at least difficult, to grind and hone. Many of us have probably showered curses on dull rust-resistant kitchen knives that were eventually shoved to the back of the knife drawer. But we forgot—or perhaps did not know—that rust-resistant steel used in kitchen knives is made from *18/8-steel*, which can't harden and is difficult to sharpen.

Today the problem of grinding and honing rust-resistant blades is no longer an issue. The use of rust-resistant steel has forced manufacturers to produce better hones. Traditionally, sandstone and slate sharpeners were worn down quickly when sharpening a rust-resistant blade. Now we have artificially made hones, including ceramic and diamond hones, which take on even the hardest steel and create a fine, sharp edge.

A rust-resistant blade is easy to manage in spite of its disadvantages. As a fishing knife it is unbeatable, particularly if it comes into contact with salt water. Many hunters are now also trying rust-resistant blades in their knives. In an emergency, such a knife can be stuffed down into the sheath full of blood or fish guts, and can be cleaned the following day without affecting the blade.

However, don't assume that steel will tolerate everything, even if it's rust-resistant. Edge steel, in particular, can rust if mistreated over a long period of time. Nonetheless, today's excellent rust-resistant steel does not have many disadvantages compared to carbonized steel. For knives that are often neglected (during hunting or fishing, for example), a rust-resistant blade is much more forgiving.

In my experience, rust-resistant blades stay sharp longer than blades made of carbonized steel. I believe many others have made the same observation, but have not dared to admit it. Steel manufacturers have done tests that show that good rust-resistant steel remains sharp longer than carbonized steel. Rust-resistance has come to stay.

THE BLADE: FORM AND FUNCTION

You will soon discover that knife blades come in nearly every shape: long, medium-long, short, narrow, wide, curved, and so on. At first, it may be difficult to know what to buy, so some explanation is appropriate here.

In general, a blade with a relatively strong curve at the tip is a good, multipurpose blade. Many everyday knives used by carpenters, hunters, and people who spend time outdoors are shaped accordingly. A common example is the classic Mora knife. A blade with this shape that is 8 to 10 cm (3 to 4 inches) long is a good first knife.

The blade for a multipurpose knife should also be rather short (Fig. 1). This makes the blade easier to control and stronger (in basic wood carving, for example). Such a knife can clean fish, as well as cut bread. It has an edge that is long enough for skinning. On the other hand, it is not a useful blade for fine wood carving.

Don't forget that there is no one knife that is perfect for every job. Watch a Sami at work. (The Sami, or Lapp, people are the indigenous inhabitants of Norway, Sweden, Finland, and the Russian Kola

Peninsula.) He may carry up to four to five different knives with him, each one suited for a special purpose.

A blade with a sharper curve at the tip is called a *skinning knife* (Fig. 2). For the most part, it can't be used for anything other than skinning roe deer and larger wild animals. The blade of a skinning knife has a *drop point* to reduce the risk of poking a hole in the stomach when the knife is turned up and down to open the abdomen (Fig. 3).

You will definitely need a blade that is designed specifically for woodworking if you are considering doing a lot of woodcarving and need to create fine details and cut strong curves (Fig. 4). The blade must be both short and very pointy to control it deftly and to reach everywhere.

There is a wide range of variations of knife blades. Most are intended exclusively for hunting and have exotic names like *clippoint, skinner, ripper*, and so on. But because they are very specialized, I will not discuss them all in detail.

Blades that are 12 to 15 cm (about 4½ to 6 inches) or longer are mainly intended for hunting. Do not make a general purpose knife out of one of these just to impress! You will soon find that such a knife is not practical in most situations.

All types of blades sometimes have a section on the edge nearest the handle that wasn't ground down evenly with the rest of the edge. It should be as short as possible (not over 5 mm or about $^{11}/_{64}$ inch) or, preferably, completely missing. Otherwise, you will lose the most important part of the blade, the part that gives the greatest strength. Also, this is the section of the blade that is often used to make chips for the fire.

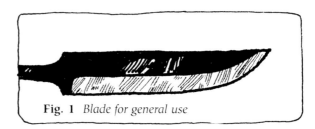

Fig. 1 *Blade for general use*

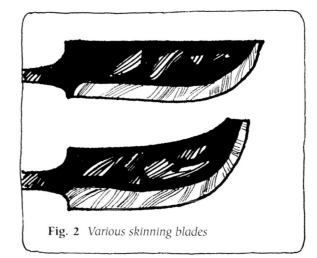

Fig. 2 *Various skinning blades*

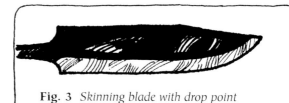

Fig. 3 *Skinning blade with drop point*

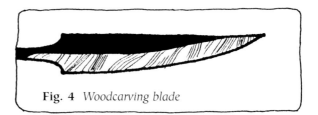

Fig. 4 *Woodcarving blade*

MATERIALS FOR HANDLES AND SHEATHS

WOOD

For your knife handle, you can use nearly any type of wood. The selection of wood determines both the appearance and strength of the knife. Even the simplest model, without decorations, can be quite beautiful if the handle is made from a striking or unusual material. Few things are more exciting for a knifemaker than sawing up the knotty growths on the trunk discovered after a hard day of searching!

But do not count on it being easy to find handle material. It will take some time to learn where to look. Knotty growths on the trunks of trees are often found in marshes along rivers, brooks, and other water courses. They are easiest to find during the winter; this is also when they have the least moisture. Other places to look are in broken-up stubs in clearings or in the fork between two strong branches on a broad-leafed tree. Do not forget to test-saw fresh stubs that look interesting.

Because a knife handle is subject to stress, it is a good idea to select harder types of wood as handles. I have used juniper, oak, and common birch, as well as beech, ash, and mountain ash. Whitebeam, maple, and most fruit trees can also be used (Fig. 5). Fruit trees and even laburnum, if you can find it, yield handles with beautiful patterns of visible annual rings and a fine contrast between heartwood and sapwood. I

think that the role of the juniper has been underrated. It is very tough and strong (with tight annual rings), has subtle color variations, and smells wonderful.

To try out a new handle model, I often cut it from completely fresh ash first. It is quick and easy work, and you will soon find out if the model will work before you use the harder wood. This has saved me numerous expensive pieces of finer wood.

Nowadays, you can purchase very beautiful pieces of wood, including scrap walnut, from rifle-butt manufacturers. It is usually sold in large, useable pieces.

I have the advantage of living in a part of southern Sweden that is rich in woodlands. Throughout the year, I take weekly walks in the woods. It has become my habit to keep an eye peeled for any type of wood that could be used for new knives. Whenever I find something interesting, I ask the locals who own the woods. I have never had a problem obtaining an interesting piece of wood for a small amount of money. I have often been given it for free when I explained what I was using it for. (I have even found new customers for my knives in this manner.) In a stack, I recently discovered a large piece of birch, half of which was of the curly grained variety. The owner allowed me to have half of the log for free. It would

Fig. 5 *Various materials for handles. From the left: two piece of curly grained birch, pine root, curly grained sallow, walnut, curly grained oak, juniper wood, and juniper root*

have been used for pulpwood otherwise. Other great finds are curly grained oak, sallow, curly grained elm, and some knotty growths on the trunk of the birch. Remember it is illegal to take live, healthy trees without asking permission.

Curly grained birch is probably the most beautiful wood for knife handles and has been used since old times (for example, by the Sami) as a material for everything from bowls to milk containers, from cheese forms to knife handles. Ladles, spoons, and thimbles are also made of knots of curly grained birch wood.

If you succeed in finding a knotty growth on the trunk of a tree with curly grained wood, such as birch, and have the permission of the owner of the tree to take it, do the following: Saw a cut directly into the straight wood a few decimeters (about 8 inches) above and below the knotty growth on the trunk. Then cut or pry the entire piece loose. The straight part of the trunk will become material for the handle. Note: *the tree does not need to be cut down.* Although it is possible to saw knotty growths into handle material for knives, you need to wait a few years until the wood dries completely before it can be used.

Curly grained birch wood is commonly used for knife handles. Unlike most other types of wood, the surface of curly grained birch does not become perforated with fibers or pores from the polished wood fibers. Instead, it becomes hard and smooth and very resistant to damage. The opposite properties can be seen in wooden oak, beech, or walnut, among others. No matter how long you polish these woods, you will never get a surface as smooth as that of curly grained wood. Instead, you get other beautiful qualities.

Curly grained wood can be purchased ready to use for handles, in pieces about 3.5 x 4.5 x 13 cm (1¼ x 1 ¾ x 5 inches), or as planking and logs. A piece of log is harder to purchase than curly grained wood in plank form and you can never tell how the log will look on the inside.

Sallow and curly grained elm are often more beautiful than curly grained birch, but they are not as strong and durable. Curly grained birch is very hard to work with, is too challenging for completely inexperienced hands, and requires very sharp tools. But it is wonderful for handles that need to withstand rough treatment. Curly grained wood is very hard to split when it is dry. The wood tolerates pressure from a twisted knife tang without splitting. Proper after-treatment results in a curly grained wood handle that becomes more beautiful with age, is nice to hold, and has good grip when it is wet. And it becomes more beautiful with repeated oilings with boiled linseed oil.

Scrap pieces of other types of wood can sometimes be obtained if you contact a woodworking teacher. Also try going to the library and reading advertisements in hunting publications that give addresses where various types of fine wood can be obtained. (Look in the "Miscellaneous" column.)

HORN

You will need reindeer horn if you are considering making an all-horn knife, or one with a mixture of horn and wood, as in the Sami model. Elk and other types of horn can also be used, but they are difficult to find.

Like curly grained wood, reindeer antlers have been used by the Sami for a long time, both for utilitarian and decorative purposes. Reindeer antlers are also used for inlaid woodwork in wooden objects. Only the antlers of the bull are good for woodworking materials, since those of the reindeer cows are too frail and twisted.

Every year, reindeer shed their antlers and grow new ones. Therefore, the quality of the antlers depends on the quality of the pasturage, above all the winter pasturage, that the reindeer find. You can use antlers from animals that were butchered and from bulls that were castrated. Working with antlers requires strong pieces of antler with little or no marrow at all. See Fig. 6.

The beautiful, curved part of the end of a Sami knife is made of *rosenkrans,* or the part of the antler that is closest to the skull on the reindeer. It is the part of the antler that has the largest diameter; it does not have marrow and is very hard, which is a prereq-

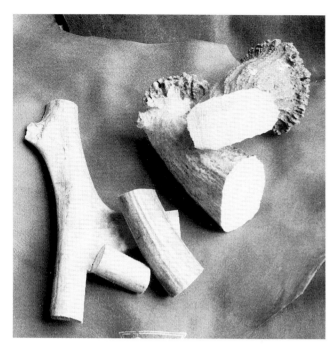

Fig. 6 *Pieces of reindeer antler (left) and elk horn (right)*

uisite for being able to rivet the tang of the knife into the back end without the antler splitting or the rivet sinking in. It is difficult to find these antler pieces, since there are only two on each reindeer.

The greenish antler that can be found in slaughter houses is wonderful for knifemaking. Yellow-colored and sun-bleached antlers are found higher up in the mountains. Beautiful marbled antlers with grey and grey-brown nuances are sometimes found at butchers. Previously, white antlers were considered the most beautiful type of antler. They turn white if you lay them out and let them bleach in the sun. You can even put them in water, in a cold spring, for example, for a long time. Today, however, white antlers are scarce. The nuances of the antler are used in combination with the veining and color variations in the wood.

The piece that is just outside the rosenkrans is also very important for the knifemaker. It is the piece that is used for the antler work on the Sami knife.

LEATHER

The most common kinds of leather for making knife sheaths are *vegetable-tanned natural leather* and *bark-tanned cowhide* or *reindeer hide*. A 2 mm ($\frac{1}{16}$ inch) thickness of leather is usually sufficient for knife sheaths.

Vegetable-tanned leather is tanned with vegetable tanning material; that is, with products from the plant kingdom, such as bark and leaves. The processes that change rawhide to leather are called *tanning*. Vegetable-tanned leather is relatively easy to work with, even for a beginner, and is free of poisonous and allergy-producing substances. It is very easy to shape and holds up well to wear and tear. It darkens with time and becomes more beautiful the more it is used. Natural vegetable-tanned leather is a prerequisite if you wish to pattern and dye your leather. (If you purchase pre-dyed leather, you have missed the opportunity to put a design on it.)

Bark-tanned cowhide or bark-tanned raw leather (Sami knife leather) is tanned in another manner. Cowhide or reindeer hide is tanned with bark from sallow, birch, willow, and alder. Birch bark creates a darker tone, while sallow produces a leather that is lighter but easier to work. Finally, the leather is colored with the inner part of the alder bark, which is ground down and rubbed out, then mixed with water and poured over the hide. The alder bark turns the leather a beautiful, deep reddish-brown color. By avoiding tanning the leather all the way through, a layer of rawhide is left in the middle. This leather makes a very hard knife sheath. The knife gets excellent protection, and the leather is very tolerant of external forces. In addition, the sheath is not damaged by the edge of the knife every time you withdraw the blade.

In terms of wear and tear, bark-tanned leather is significantly better than vegetable-tanned leather. The disadvantage is that, for a beginner, it is harder to work. It requires strong pinching and really good softening before it can be shaped. Therefore, I would recommend that you begin with the vegetable-tanned leather; then, after you gain more experience, try bark-tanned leather.

13

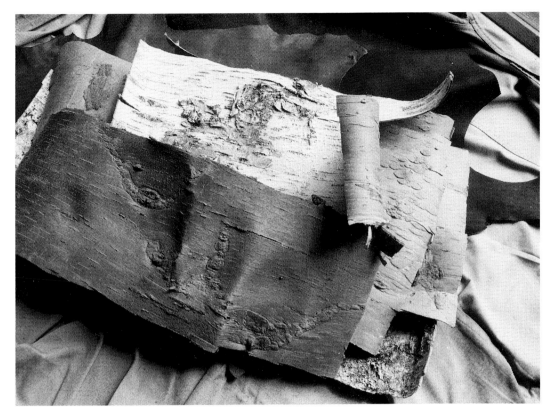

Fig. 7 *Birch bark from various* Betula pubescens *birch trees*

Some knifemakers tan their own leather, but since it is time consuming, it is not the place to start. If you wish to try tanning at some point, there are some excellent books available on the subject. I have only briefly touched on the subject of tanning here, because there are so many other things that need to be mastered first.

Sinew thread is the strongest thread to use to sew leather sheaths. It is made from the sinews in the back (along the saddle) and legs of a reindeer. Most commonly, sinew thread comes from the front side of the legs.

All leather is measured in square feet. A square foot of leather is the surface of a square with sides measuring just over 30 cm (12 inches). The finished hide is divided in the middle, partly because it is more practical to work with that way. If you need more than a square foot, you can often buy ¼, ½, or a whole section of a side. The leather will be cheaper the larger the piece you buy at one time.

BIRCH BARK

As a knifemaker, you may need birch bark. It makes an excellent material for evening out the parts of a Sami knife. If you want to make a knife sheath completely of birch bark, high-quality birch bark is a prerequisite. Shredded or powdered bark (either birch or alder) can be used to color in the scratches you cut into a horn sheath. Mix the powder with linseed oil or saliva, then stroke the mixture on with your fingertips and allow to dry.

You should collect birch bark when the trees have sap in the spring. It is dried in layers in the air under the weight of logs or stones. If you want to collect your own birch bark, but are not allowed to take it from live trees, try taking it from cut birch trees that are stacked up. It is easiest to get the birch bark loose in the spring—when it has sap. Birch bark is tougher and more resistant in fall and winter, but harder to get loose. Do not take the bark that is underneath,

14

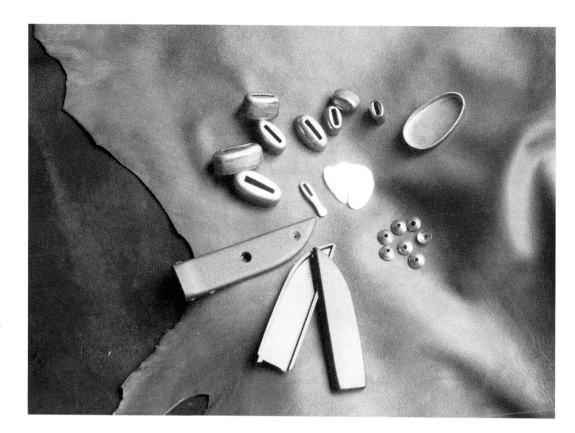

Fig. 8 *Clockwise from the bottom center: knife edge guards, ferrules, top plates, rivet washers. In the middle: finger protector and tin spacers.*

only the outer bark. Try collecting it just after the end of a cold spell. Large flakes of birch bark will come loose from the bark underneath if long vertical cuts are made with a sharp knife. If it does not tear loose on its own, move your hand around the trunk to help loosen it. See Fig. 7.

Again, if you are only allowed to take birch that has already been cut, it is easiest to loosen in the spring. The trunk has sap even though the birch has been cut. But this is only true for a short while; therefore, it is best to go and check every day to help loosen it. NOTE: *Taking birch bark without the permission of the owner is not allowed.*

OTHER MATERIALS

In addition to the materials I have already mentioned, you will also need hollow punches, hole punches, edge cutters, trimming wood, leather glue, flaking knives, hammers and mallets, steel rulers, cut-ting boards, belt cutters, pricking irons, thonging chisels, scrap leather, leather punches, oil for leather and leather grease, harrow blacking, leather dye, O-rings and D-rings, hand tools for pipe rivets, and eyelets. Aluminum and brass plates in various thicknesses are available from hardware stores and scrap metal companies. See Fig. 8 for additional hardware you will need for knifemaking.

Purchasing a complete knife-building kit is an excellent beginning to your knifemaking career. Kits include all the materials you need and are available in several levels of difficulty.

All materials should be of the best quality, whether it be wood, horn, leather, or anything else. This is a prerequisite for producing quality knives, with respect to both appearance and durability.

Fig. 9 *Knifemaking tools: 1. Epoxy glue (or two-component adhesive glue); 2. Wood cement; 3. Masking tape; 4. Coping saw; 5. Mini hacksaw; 6. Hacksaw; 7. Half-round file (cabinet file); round file; rasping file; 8. Bar-clamp; 9. Glue clamps; 10. Bow saw clamp; 11. High-speed steel drill bits (1-10 mm or ⅟₃₂-⅜ in.); 12. Deep throat fret saw; 13. Screwdrivers; 14. Caliper; 15. Awl; 16. Manual drill or brace with auger bit; 17. Ball peen hammer; 18. Rubber mallet; 19. Wood chisel; 20. Mora knife; 21. Steel or aluminum ruler*

TOOLS FOR MAKING KNIVES

You probably already have many of the tools you will need for knifemaking at home in your tool drawer and are already familiar with how to use them (Fig. 9). Do not let yourself be convinced that the road to your dream knife is paved with a gigantic collection of tools and aids. Have a little patience and let time determine your needs. Learn to use the tools that you already have more effectively,

and discover the special features of each tool. You will be amazed at what these faithful servants can accomplish.

If you don't have a lot of tools—perhaps you haven't done woodworking since you were in school—sit down and think! You probably have a friend, colleague, or neighbor who has tools he or she doesn't use very often that you can borrow until you can buy your own. When you do have money to spend, you will have a better idea of which brands you work well with. If you need almost everything, why not ask the shop teacher at the local school? Perhaps it would even be possible to use your local school workshop in the evenings or on weekends.

It is important to remember to focus on quality when you are purchasing new tools or materials. The expense will be higher, but you will get back every penny in good work and loyal service. Avoid buying a complete set of woodworking tools for decorating your knives. Get one or two really useful, high-quality tools instead. Many tool sets look impressive and perhaps strengthen your self confidence for a while, but quantity destroys inventiveness and creativity. Use your best tools—and your head and your hands—to find solutions.

THE PRIMARY TOOLS

You will need some drill bits with accompanying drill shanks or a brace with auger bits. Of course, the best and most effective drilling tool is a power drill. A hacksaw with blades is useful for metal work. A mini hacksaw is very cheap and also very useful. (Make sure you get blades for both wood and metal.) You will need a hacksaw to make a Sami knife with a horn sheath and a fret saw and a jigsaw with blades for working with metal and wood. A ball peen hammer is used for riveting work. A double-grade half-round file is helpful if you can afford it and a rasp helps smooth rough wood and horn.

Other tools that will come in handy are a regular screwdriver, a very small screwdriver, an awl handle with round and square awls, a Mora knife, and a gauge. You will need a variety of clamps: 30-mm (about 1-inch) clamps, some glue clamps, and a couple of fret-saw clamps. Masking tape protects the knife blade while you work.

A ruler is helpful, preferably one with a steel edge. You will also want to have wood cement and epoxy glue, a wood chisel (about 10 mm or about $\frac{3}{8}$ inch wide), a lead pencil, sandpaper (up to 320-grit for a smooth finish), a jaw vise, some very fine copper wire, and a wooden or rubber mallet. You may also need a sliding caliper, one or more tapered files, and a small craft knife. Some rotating rasp attachments for a power drill come in handy for working with wood.

TOOLS FOR LEATHER WORK

In this section, I discuss the tools you will need for working with leather to make knife sheaths. Not many tools are needed, so don't worry. As is the case with woodworking tools, you probably already have some of them. Perhaps you should borrow the tools for the leather work if you intend to make only a few occasional knife sheaths. See Fig. 11.

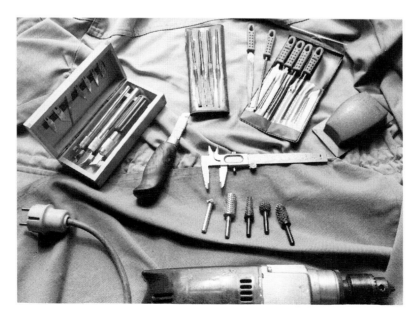

Fig. 10 *Tools that you will need (from left): hobby knives with various blades, assorted tapered files, fine-threaded files for wood and metal, tripod stand, sliding caliper, rotating rasps and files for wood (bottom center), and a power drill*

17

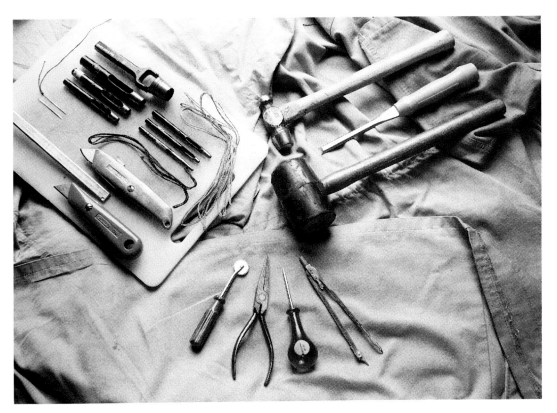

Fig. 11 *Tools for working with leather (from left): cutting board, utility knives, steel ruler, pitch thread, saddler's needles, hollow punches, hammer, wood chisel rubber mallet, caliper, awl, long-nose pliers, and pricking wheel*

You will need a steel or wooden ruler with a steel edge. It must be a maximum of 30 cm (12 inches) long if you only need it for leather sheaths. Plastic rulers can't tolerate the force necessary to cut leather. In a short time, the entire ruler will become jagged and you can slip and injure your fingers. Sandpaper glued on the back of your ruler will keep it in position.

A utility knife with an interchangeable blade is the only type of knife that has enough firmness to cut into leather. A straight, standard blade is very good for cutting, but use a cutting board. Retractable knives with interchangeable blades are unfortunately too weak for leather. You will need a stiff (non-twisting) blade; it also needs to be as thin as possible.

You probably already have a plastic/nylon cutting board. This is an excellent cutting board for knifemaking. Make sure that all the grease has been thoroughly washed off. A cutting board is very important, since it will help your tools last significantly longer. Even a layer of wood or cork underneath works well.

A caliper will help you measure distances, mark the seams, and mark the curves. Get a caliper with an adjustable screw that keeps the caliper open.

A mallet is used to pound the leather tools, primarily the hollow punches. A plastic, nylon, or rubber mallet works, but the best (and most expensive) kind is a rawhide mallet. Be careful when using common metal hammers with hollow punches and wood chisels; hammers made of metal destroy the heads of the tools very quickly.

To make holes, you will need round hollow punches. Rotating punch tongs can also be used, but they can only reach easily accessible places. I use only hollow punches of various dimensions, from about 2 mm to 25 mm ($\frac{1}{16}$ to about 1 inch inch). Begin with a maximum of three sizes and complement with other sizes later. To make really nice-looking holes, spend the money on hollow punches. Use the cutting board as a work surface, and pound with the mallet from straight above. If the leather circles get stuck in them, I remove them with steel wire. If you need a rectangular hole, make two holes with the hollow punch and remove the leather between them with chisels. Rectangular hollow punches exist, but are expensive.

You will need a sharp chisel around 10 mm (about ⅜ inch) wide for some leatherwork and a regular hammer to pound the rivets together. A couple of size 3 saddler's needles are necessary for making saddler's stitches at the back of the leather sheaths. These needles are blunt, because you sew in ready-made holes. An awl, preferably with interchangeable tips, is also a good tool to have. A leather awl is not round, but rather flattened and rectangular.

In addition, you will need thread for sewing the leather. Sinew thread is the strongest and best thread—and the most expensive. Pitched thread is probably the most common. It comes colored either natural or black.

You can put pitch on the thread yourself, if you don't want to buy already-pitched thread. It is very easy. Buy a roll of linen thread (18/3 or 20/3) and a piece of black or yellow wax pitch. Heat the pitch a little over a heat source, then pull the linen thread through the wax pitch. Rubbing the linen thread with a bit of leather so that the friction raises the temperature of the thread also works well; do this before you pull the thread through the wax. Remember that black pitch thread easily comes off and discolors natural leather.

Linen thread is also good for sewing leather. You can purchase it with or without wax treatment, though it is easier to sew with wax-treated thread. Purchase a cake of beeswax. Heat the wax and pull the linen thread through the wax, even if the thread has already been treated with wax. Wipe off the excess. A suitable thickness of linen thread is 18/3. (Eighteen is the thickness of the thread, and three indicates that the thread is twined with three strands.)

Leather can be sewn with many things—everything from dental floss to metal wire to embroidery yarn. The three threads I have mentioned are the most common. A pricking wheel easily pokes holes quickly and exactly where you want to sew, giving the same distance between the thread holes.

A pair of long-nosed pliers with long, flat jaws can be used to pull a needle through a crooked hole while sewing or to pull out old rivets.

There is a whole world of useful tools and aids for working with leather. The ones mentioned above are the ones I use nearly every time I make a sheath or part of a sheath. It is difficult to exclude any of them.

Some additional items you might include on your wish list are: an edge beveler, a belt cutter, a thonging chisel, some scrap bolt needles, punches, a snap-fastener tool, a bone folder, and a tripod. But only the future will tell you exactly what you need.

YOUR WORK SPACE

You will not need much space to make your knife. Nearly any small room or corner will work. I have never had an actual workshop, instead I made my knives in a little 1.5 x 1.5 m (5 x 5 feet) washroom. It has actually been quite easy to work among laundry baskets and drying clothing—with an understanding family.

You need a work table in any case. A real carpenter's bench has long been on my wish list, but I manage well with a small folding bench. It is versatile and serves all the functions of a large bench. When folded up, it takes up almost no room. By sweeping or vacuuming the floor after each job, the room is kept navigable.

It is important to have a good light source, either a good, movable work lamp with a bright light or a reliable window. A garbage can and space for your tools is also important. It is nice to have a place to store your tools if you really want order in your work area. That way, your tools are protected and easy to find. I use a paper or pen stand with a pigeon hole in it, which is cheap, but very practical. You can also nail small pieces of leather on the walls, using two nails for each piece. Make the area that hangs down between the nails an appropriate size for various tools. Count on small gadgets and devices being added later on. Linseed oil, turpentine, leather dye, and so on, are stored in a cupboard.

You will need an airy space with an even temperature in which to store the wood so the wood won't split. For those of us who collect materials ourselves, the long drying time and the risk of splitting are disadvantages we have to deal with. Do not try to dry any wood at room temperature or at any higher temperatures! My pieces are allowed to dry out on the porch under a roof for approximately six months. A cellar/basement is also a good drying place, provided it's not damp and very little sunlight comes in. Grease the surface of all the pieces with a thick layer of regular wood cement, but don't remove the bark.

After six to nine months, you can bring the wood inside, but keep checking it. Put the pieces back out again immediately if you discover signs of splitting and give them an extra layer of wood cement. A few months later, you can attempt to bring them in again. If everything goes well, you can saw the materials in pieces approximately 3 to 4 cm (1¼ to 1½ inch) thick and finish drying them that way.

Stack up the pieces of wood so that air can circulate between each layer. Then, by weighing each piece, you can determine when the moisture content has stabilized. Should you become too impatient and take a piece in too early, your knife handle will eventually split. A quick method I learned from the Sami is to boil knotty growths or other materials in lightly salted water for approximately two hours. (The larger the piece, the longer it takes.) Break or cut off all the bark. While boiling, the sap is drawn out of the wood and the risk of splitting is reduced. After boiling, grease the surfaces again with wood cement. It is best to cut the wood roughly before boiling it. Collect all wood during the winter (when it contains the least sap), then let it dry slowly.

When I first started making knives, I tried to reduce the risk of splitting by wrapping the wood in plastic bags. This just caused the wood to get moldy, become discolored, and smell awful. When I then dried it in the usual manner, the discoloration remained all the way through the wood pattern, giving a very unusual and beautiful character to otherwise uniform wood; but be careful to stop the discoloration before it reaches the roots.

Leather and the things that go with it, like pitch thread, sinew thread, needles, and so on, are in a special corner in my workroom. The leather does best if it is rolled together, preferably around an empty paper-towel roll. This is to prevent the leather from folding or bending and getting marks that will never go away. Do not let the leather sit in the sunlight; it stains the surface.

The only problem with my workbench is that it is too weak to hold a vise. I solved this problem by using a chopping block, about 1 m (3¼ feet) high, which I have stored outside. It is easy to bring in when I need to rivet a knife tang or clamp together a leather rivet.

A FEW ADDITIONAL WORDS

More so in the past than today, the knife was a multi-purpose tool that was treated like a prized possession. It was used for a long time and sometimes even passed down from father to son. When I hold a knife in my hands, I can't help but think back to the person who made it. I do not think the knifemaker thought much about earning money when making it. Perhaps it was made to serve a specific urgent need, or to give to some friend or relative.

Regardless of the reason for making the knife, the satisfaction of having successfully produced something that is both useful and beautiful lies deep in the heart of the knifemaker. Traditionally, the knife was not a consumer product that was made hastily. The knifemaker worked on it as long as necessary. If a day or week wasn't long enough, they took two weeks or a month. They worked with it, twisted and turned it, and looked at it from thousands of angles so that it not only became useful, but also beautiful. A knife was a piece of long-lasting love hidden in a useful gift for someone else, the finest gift a person can get.

When the knife was designed, the knifemaker built on the traditions from his father and grandfather. It is something of this old spirit and attitude that I wish for modern knifemakers. I wish for you the ability to work for the sake of desire and pleasure, for the joy of discovery and the satisfaction of having produced something with your own hands that is useful in daily life. It is a journey of discovery, and I wish for you to do your very best.

Once you discover the joy of knifemaking, you will become skilled. If you love the work, you will gradually become a fine knifemaker. You will not have good results if you have no feeling for what you are doing. It's the difference between a wooden stick with a piece of sheet metal in it, and a work of art. Don't give up because you think everything is going badly at first. Go away for an hour or even a few days. Try again, and the knowledge you have will grow with you. Be patient with yourself, and the results will come.

Lars Piraks, a Sami woodworker, in his book *Sameslöjd* [Sami Woodworking], says:

"I have many half-finished objects in my studio. The products must dry properly, and I prefer to become familiar with the lumps of materials. Sometimes I pick up the half-finished object and look at its structure and form. It is allowed to sit for a few more months. Perhaps I will discover some detail in the graining or veining of the wood that I will use in the composition. One day, perhaps after some years, I begin to work the piece of material. I sharpen my tools. The knotty growths from the trunk of the birch often require time and strength. The sweat runs and the palms of my hands feel warm. The chopping of the ax echoes dully and the wood flakes fall like leaves to the floor. Previously, before drying, I have roughly cut the knotty growth from the birch trunk, so that it is half-finished, and boiled it in reindeer bullion. Now it is a matter of a more refined repetition of carving. Time after time, I interrupt the work and think and observe the forms of nature. How does this piece of work tempt me? Should I use its detailed shapes or wood grain to get the right tension in the final lines and give life to the object? It is difficult, but it

makes the work interesting. My sketchbook comes out and I work with a pencil and make idea sketches. It is easier to make mistakes with the pencil, because you can throw away the piece of paper. You can't make a mistake with the shape of the wood, because it's hard to correct the mistake. The object must have freedom and vitality in it. Preferably, it should reflect something of the spiritual life and the pleasure the maker takes in the work. I come to a halt, and my thoughts go to the beautiful world of the mountains and nature where I got the object: birds, animal life, legends, and being around people . . . form a certain sublevel in my creation of forms."

These are the thoughts of a woodworker shaping the final object. Later, he writes:

"The materials for its structure are so different. The woodworker must be sensitive to many things, most of all of the material. Sensitive to the soul and sensitive with the eyes and fingertips. It is a matter of giving the object its final touch.

Gentle polishing or surface treatment can be enough to reach rest and tension in the final lines of the finished object. The woodworking object is ready to be used or sold. It is a satisfaction that is deeply felt by the woodworker to have completed something. A simple pleasure—that everyday moment of satisfaction. In reality, it is just a link in the chain towards increasingly new and higher goals. I continually strive to increase the quality, renew, and discover daring manipulation of the material that can allow greater and more meaningful artistic expression. It takes time and perhaps it requires more ability for discovery on the part of the observer and by the person who uses the object."

There is no better way to say it!

PREPARING THE KNIFE BLADE

Now that you have gathered all the tools and materials you will need to make a knife, the next section describes several ways of making knife handles, with step-by-step instructions.

Before you begin to make the handle, you must inspect the knife blade. You must respect it. It is often wrapped or has a taped edge, but it can also come without protection. Remove the shipping tape from your blade and inspect it. Look at the edge. Check to make sure that there aren't any notches or other damage to the blade. Ask to exchange the blade for a different one if you do find faults in it.

If you have purchased a laminated blade, make sure that it really is laminated. Hold the blade so that a light source falls against the sharp part of the blade.

Begin by looking at the short end of the blade to see if there are any faint wavy lines a few millimeters (1/16 inch) from the edge that go from the short side of the blade to the point. Sometimes they are hard to find. There may be a change in the gray shade on the polished surface (Fig. 1).

At some point, the blade ends and a narrower part called the tang of the knife begins. This is the part of the blade that will lie hidden in the handle. Though the width of the tang varies, you will discover that it is narrowest at the end of the handle that is farthest from the blade—where the stress is the greatest (Fig. 2). A thick and broad blade is very wide at the top. This is so that it can absorb more of the turning power of the blade. Most knife tangs

Fig. 1

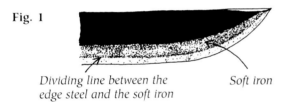

Dividing line between the edge steel and the soft iron   *Soft iron*

Fig. 2 *Knife tang*

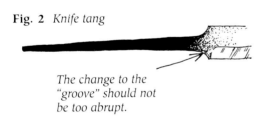

The change to the "groove" should not be too abrupt.

A broad blade should have a broader groove.

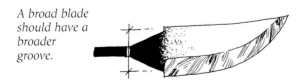

A Roselli blade has a round tang that is welded on.

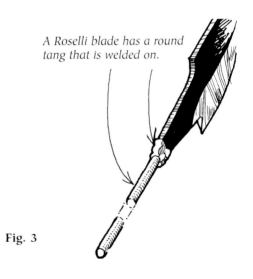

Fig. 3

Fig. 4   *Don't forget to tape the blade.*

are rectangular in the cross section. But there are blades that have a round tang (for example, Roselli blades). A round staff of softer metal has been welded to this type of blade (Fig. 3).

Wrap the blade with masking tape again, preferably two layers thick to prevent you (or the blade) from being injured while you work (Fig. 4). Also wrap a couple of layers across the blade at the back end. This will prevent you from spilling epoxy glue on the blade and scratching it when you attempt to scrape the glue off.

Some important things to remember when making knives:

- ► Use first-class components.
- ► Practice accuracy and patience.
- ► Be a careful planner—do everything in the proper order.
- ► Never mess with the surface treatment.
- ► Use sharp tools.

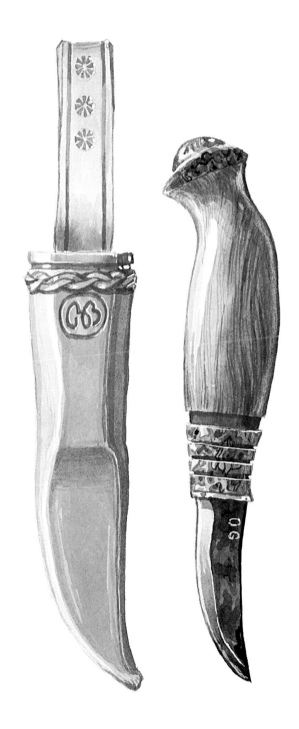

Small, multipurpose game knife (right): The front part of the handle is curly grained birch, the back is selected juniper wood; the blade is hand-forged and hand-welded. The all-leather sheath was made using the knife as a model (left).

ALL-WOOD HANDLES

urly grained birch is used for this knife. When looking for wood, make sure that you don't get any branches in the pieces of wood. (Sometimes they can only be seen on one side.) If you do, simply cut off that part. Look at the ends to see if there is any splitting that can go halfway through the piece. See page 87 for a color photograph of an all-wood handle.

SKETCHING AND PLANNING THE HANDLE

Begin this project by planning the handle. A narrow handle is hard to hold with a wet hand. Even if you think that you have a clear picture of how the handle should look, begin by sketching it on a piece of paper (preferably greaseproof paper) at full scale (Fig. 1). I have made an accurate sketch of each one of the

knives I have approved. It may seem unnecessary, but when you start sawing and shaping the material for the handle, it is very easy to lose the image that was so clear when you started. Then you will have to improvise to correct your mistakes; and the resulting handle is often completely different from what you imagined—and sometimes completely useless. Use black lead and keep changing the sketch until you are satisfied. Remember that the handle must fit in your hand and be long enough.

I use greaseproof paper for two reasons: 1) If you lay a sketch on top of the handle material, the pattern and graining of the wood show through. Thus, you can easily decide where on the piece the handle will be sawed out. 2) The loose blade can be placed beneath the sketch to see how the blade and handle model fit together.

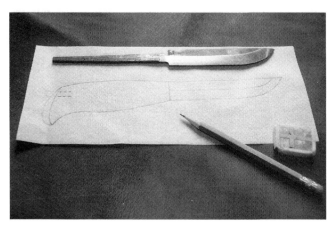

Fig. 1 *Sketch the knife at full scale on greaseproof paper.*

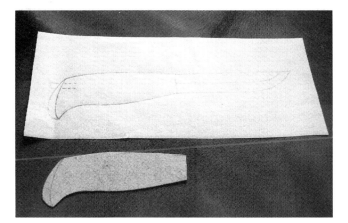

Fig. 2 *Make a cardboard model of the handle.*

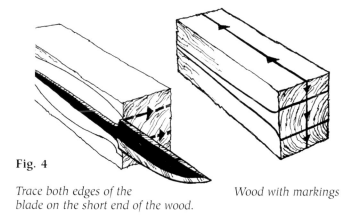

5 mm (approx. ¹¹/₆₄ in.)

At least 5 mm (approx ¹¹/₆₄ in.) must stick out at the back

Fig. 3

Cut along the dotted line.

Fig. 4

Trace both edges of the blade on the short end of the wood.   *Wood with markings*

Curly grained wood is a common handle material and is usually approximately 3.5 x 4.5 x 13 cm (about 1½ x 1¾ x 5 inches). Use the entire piece for the handle. Excess scrap material is useable, but can yield false gains trying to get good leftover pieces from the beginning.

If you are still a little doubtful as to how the knife will feel in your hand, do this: transfer the sketch to a piece of cardboard (Fig. 2). Use carbon paper or push hard with the pencil and cut out a cardboard replica of the handle. Errors that are not seen on the sketch are often discovered in this way.

When I make a new and possibly unusual model, I take an additional step. I take a piece of fresh aspen or some other type of soft wood and cut a rough model out of it. It doesn't take long, but allows the volume of the handle to be felt. This has saved me a lot of

cursing and a lot of expensive wood!

Next, take the piece of wood, and twist and turn it a little. Where is the most beautiful pattern, the most original grain? Very seldom do you get a piece with fine, tight curly grained wood all the way through. Instead, you must decide which side of the knife will be the most beautiful. Hold the greaseproof paper up to the wood. How does the wood look between the contours? NOTE: Make sure that the tang is longer than the handle. At least 5 mm (¹¹/₆₄ inch) needs to stick out the back (Fig. 3).

When you decide which section of the wood piece works best, take the cardboard model and trace the contours of the sides of the handle on it. Cut along the dotted line, leaving a margin of a few millimeters (¹/₁₆ inch). Use a fine-ended saw, and make sure that

25

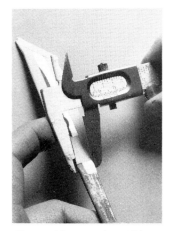

Fig. 5 *Measure the width of the tang.*

Fig. 6 *Mark the entry hole for the blade.*

DRILLING HOLES FOR THE TANG

Take a drill bit that is exactly as wide as the tang is broad and drill a hole above and below the marks. The upper drill hole must follow the contours of the tang that you drew on the long side, and the drill bit needs to exit in the midline on the other short end. Sound difficult? It is tricky at first, so follow the instructions precisely.

you don't saw at an angle (see Fig. 3). Put a piece of sandpaper on a sanding block and sand all the way down to the line.

Now push the knife tang hard against the side of the wood exactly at the right place on the handle. Take a pencil and draw along the knife tang with thick dotted lines (Fig. 4, page 25). Draw a line in from the upper and lower edges of the blade on the short end of the wood. Then make a vertical line across the entire short end. In the middle of the short end, draw a line horizontally towards the previous one. The piece of wood should now look like the one in Fig. 4 (right).

Take a ruler or a slide caliper and measure the thickness of the tang all the way to the point at which it meets the blade (Fig. 5). Mark that width on the short end of the piece of wood (Fig. 6). When you are finished, the short end should look approximately like Fig. 7. The tang of the knife must go exactly where the mark is.

Fig. 7

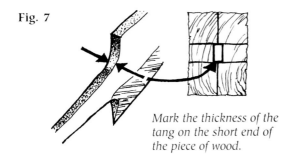

Mark the thickness of the tang on the short end of the piece of wood.

Drill the hole into the front end of the handle material with a drill bit of the same diameter as the blade is thick (a), then drill the exit hole for the tang in the back end of the handle material (b).

Fig. 8a

Fig. 8b

26

Fig. 9 *There is still room for the handle if a drill hole goes crooked.*

The front, short end

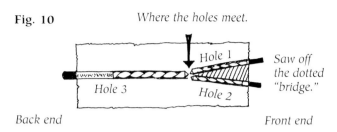

Fig. 10   *Where the holes meet.*

Hole 1

Hole 3

Hole 2

Saw off the dotted "bridge."

Back end

Front end

Use an awl to mark where you are going to put the drill bit. Take the loose drill bit between your fingers and rotate it a few times on the markings so that you can more easily find it when the drill bit is in the brace or the power drill. Begin with the upper hole. Put the tip of the drill bit in the small cavity you made in the wood. Put pressure on the brace or the power drill. Attempt to align it by sight. Alternate glances between the two long sides and adjust them by feel. Hold it still in position and begin to drill. Drill as far down as you can, even to the drill bit holder (Fig. 8a). (If you feel unsure, practice aligning on a piece of board first.) Then switch and do the same with the lower drill holes. You will soon discover that the drill doesn't reach through to the other side, since drill bits this size are not long. Drill from the other side so that the holes meet. When drilling from the back side, you need to switch to a thicker drill bit, one that is as thick as the knife tang is wide (Fig. 8b).

If you drill with a power drill, you will notice something. When you begin, there will be a sort of recoil, which causes a start for a few tenths of a second. Sometimes this is enough to cause the drill bit to hop out of its position, and the drill hole ends up a little crooked (Fig. 9). That is why I recommend using the entire piece of handle material for the handle. This gives you some margin in the wood in case the drill hole enters a little bit wrong. There is enough wood for the entire handle, even if it turns out like the Fig. 9. As far as using the thick drill bit from the back, never try to do it directly. In nine out of ten cases, it goes crooked and everything is ruined. If it is 8 mm (⁵⁄₁₆ inch) for example, drill with a 4-mm (about ⁵⁄₃₂-inch) drill bit first, then bore with a 6-mm bit (¹⁵⁄₆₄-inch), and finally with an 8-mm (⁵⁄₁₆-inch) drill bit.

Now onwards! On the back side of the handle material, you should have a bridge of wood remaining (Fig. 10) between the small drill holes. Put a loose jigsaw or bow saw blade through one hole and saw off the bridge so that the hole becomes rectangular (Fig. 11).

Next, try to insert the knife tang (Fig. 12). File the hole with a tapered file until the knife can go almost all the way in. It is a good idea to burn the hole with a hot piece of iron if possible. Assume that there is about 1 cm (⅜ inch) left before the blade meets the wood. Check to see if it is very sluggish in the last part. Push the tang in and out a few times. The hole is still too tight if all your strength is needed to move it inward a couple of millimeters (¹⁄₁₆ inch). File a little more. Try and see where on the tang it hits the wood. That is where it is tight. Now there are only a few half centimeters left (approximately ¼ inch) before it is all the way in. The tang has to be pushed in with force, but should not sit so tightly that it can't be pulled out again. If that is the case, clamp the knife blade while it is in a vise.

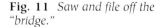

Fig. 11 *Saw and file off the "bridge."*

Fig. 12 *Test the fit of the tang.*

GLUING THE TANG

Next, mix a batch of epoxy glue. Fill the hole for the tang with glue before finally attaching the tang to the handle. You can use liquefied shellac instead. The advantage of using shellac is that, by just warming the blade, you can get the lacquer to soften so that you can take it out again. This may be necessary, for example, if your blade is badly damaged and needs to be replaced. No matter which method you prefer, it is very important that the tang fits tightly into the handle, particularly where the blade is attached. The blade must sit completely stable in the handle. If the blade is not snug, hygiene will become critical; if there is the slightest play or gap, meat, fish residue, or blood can get in, and the handle will rot and can even cause bad poisoning.

At this point, once the glue has hardened or the lacquer has stiffened, the blade should sit securely in the handle as if it has been welded into place. If the opening where the blade is attached is a little too large or wide, you can make small wood or bone wedges and tap them in on each side of the blade. Tap them

Fig. 13

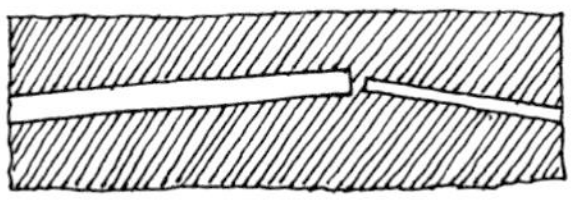

Handle material viewed from above

into place right after you pound the tang into place, but before the glue manages to harden. You only have a few minutes, so make some extra wedges in case something breaks off. Put a wood splinter on each side so that the blade is not damaged. Then hammer the piece of wood from above with a rubber mallet, so that the end of the blade is pushed in more quickly and deeply. You can hit as hard as necessary. The blade should now be in place. With correct measurements, the knife tang will stick out at least 5 mm ($\frac{11}{64}$ inch) from the back end.

If you don't succeed with the drilling, and the drill holes meet askew (a very common mistake), the following will happen: the knife tang will be forced to bend a little where the drill holes meet in order to get through (Fig. 13). You won't notice anything at that time, but

Fig. 14

once you have shaped the handle of the knife, the blade will lean a little to one direction or the other. From above, the knife will look like Fig. 14 (exaggerated). Therefore, the importance of precision drilling can not be stressed enough. Nowadays, there is a special water level you can buy that keeps the drill absolutely straight. But don't forget that you must also check to see that the handle is straight by using another level.

The very few and often abbreviated descriptions of knifemaking I have managed to find say approximately: "Drill holes in the piece/pieces so that the tang of the knife fits in there. Push in the piece/pieces, let them get a little stiff, then glue them together." My response to this method is: Don't use it! I did it as a test on ten knives of various models, using several kinds of wood. I tested everything from wood cement and contact adhesive to epoxy glue. All drying times and hardening times were followed, and the fits were perfect. Then I took them out into the woods and carved shavings for the fire. All I did was make a hole with the knives; the knives broke and were completely useless. In the knives that I made a rectangular hole in the first piece for the tang, the piece stayed. All the others came loose. Despite strong riveting, they eventually came apart; it took some a minute and some a week. (More about this in the section about handles for Sami knives.)

If you think I am too detailed, consider the results: Up to this point, I have never broken a knife that was made using my technique. The tang sits absolutely immobile up to at least half of the handle. Either the entire knife must be cracked, or very strong force is needed before it will give way.

RIVETING THE TANG INTO THE HANDLE

I almost always recommend a tang that goes all the way through (i.e., one that goes through the entire handle and is riveted at the back). I do this to make knives as strong as possible, and to emphasize strength rather than appearance. The shorter the tang, the greater the risk that the blade will come loose. Certainly there is a small danger for rust in riveting, but a few drops of oil or lacquer will prevent rusting. It is fine to glue, rivet, or screw a plate of horn or wood over the top of the rivet if you want it hidden. It is easiest if the back end has a level surface around the head of the rivet. Make a hollow in the plate to hide the head of the rivet.

The knife needs to be riveted before you begin to shape the handle. Use a jigsaw to saw off a piece of wood around the place you are going to rivet (Fig. 15). Rivet with a rivet washer. The rivet should be approximately 10 mm (about ⅜ inch) wide and slightly conical, with a hole in the middle. Brace the rivet washer in a screw vise, for example, and file a rectangular hole in it, using a tapered file the same size as the cross section on the knife tang. Slip the rivet washer over the tang and tape the washer to the wood with a couple of pieces of tape (Fig. 16). Saw off the knife tang, using a hacksaw so that only 1 mm (about ¹⁄₃₂) sticks out above the rivet washer. Brace the blade carefully in the screw vise (with some wood on each side for protection).

Then take the ball peen hammer and begin to pound (Fig. 17). Attempt to strike the ball against the middle of the end of the tang that sticks out. Try to aim the ball at the end of the knife while pounding.

Fig. 15 *Saw off a piece of wood where you are going to rivet.*

Fig. 16 *Tape the washer to the wood with a couple of pieces of tape.*

You don't need to hit hard. After a while, you will see how the end flattens out and begins to swell out over the rivet washer. When the rivet moves so that it completely covers the space between the tang and the rivet washer, tidy up the edges by pounding with the ball peen hammer.

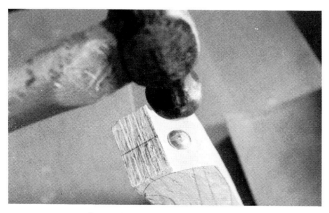

Fig. 17 *Rivet the end of the tang against the rivet washer with the ball peen hammer.*

Depending on how hard the iron is in the tang, it takes varying amounts of time to rivet. It can take from a few minutes to what feels like an eternity before you are finished. Usually it's painless, but there are some blades (for example Mora blades) with hardened tangs in which a sledge hammer is needed. In my experience, the Roselli blade, with its round tang, is the easiest, followed by other hand-forged blades. The hardest blades of all to rivet are the factory-made ones. As with everything else—be patient!

The rivet head pulls the blade towards itself and is anchored fast to the handle of the knife. Rivet some more if, contrary to expectations, there is some play after a few years. Tap in the middle of the rivet head as usual and keep at it until the blade sits fast again. The problem may be caused by slipshod sawing around the handle opening when you made the handle. Perhaps the saw "nibbled" around the edge of the opening, or the hole for the tang was a little too large. To solve the problem, rivet again, but first put the wedge between two thin, hard wooden wedges, one on each side of the blade. Alternately push the first piece with some flat object and pound the wedges with the hammer until the wedges stop and possibly break off. Tidy up with a mini hacksaw that has a fine-toothed blade. Make sure that the knife blade is protected first.

Now you have finished the hard part. If you got little annoyed by all the measuring and filing, remember that the fun part begins now. Take breaks when you need to and have fun!

29

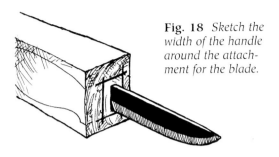

Fig. 18 *Sketch the width of the handle around the attachment for the blade.*

Fig. 19 *The top and bottom of the handle have been sawed out.*

SHAPING THE HANDLE

First, sketch the width of the handle around the attachment for the blade (Fig. 18). The contours will fade away the more you work. Clamp the handle piece and begin to saw out the handle along to the contours with a jigsaw. Begin at the front and go to the back on both sides (Fig. 19). The handle should be generally rectangular. Then mark approximately how thick the handle will be at the very front. Try to keep the saw at the same level all the time. Do not wiggle up and down.

Then begin to saw off above and below the blade. When it is ready, you will mark the midline of the handle on the upper and lower sides. Then sketch how the handle should look from above and below. Sketch loosely and then fill in the lines when the shape is clearer (Fig. 20).

Rasp the top and bottom so that both are smooth and parallel and follow the contours of the handle (Fig. 21). Then saw off the side pieces (Fig. 22). Be careful to maintain a good margin when sawing. It is better to take off too little than too much.

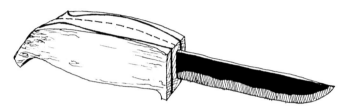

Fig. 20 *Mark the middle and outer contours of the handle on the top and bottom.*

Fig. 21 *Smooth out the sawed edges with a rasp so that they will be parallel and follow the contours of the handle.*

30

Your knife now has an angular handle. You should begin to see how it will look when it is finished. The next step is to remove the four longitudinal corners with a rasp or a knife (see Fig. 24). From above, the knife should now look approximately like the one in Fig. 23.

Make the shape increasingly round (Fig. 25). For the hard-to-reach places, you may need to use a pointed woodworking knife instead of the rasp. Mark an "x" on the highest point of the long side. Do the same for the upper and lower sides. This will prevent

Fig. 23

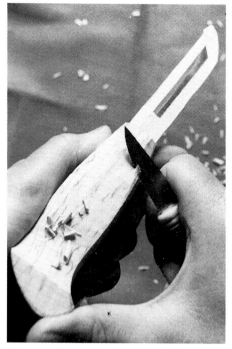

Fig. 24 *Remove the longitudinal corners.*

you from removing too much in the wrong places. Hold the knife under a bright light. Rotate the knife slowly on its longitudinal axis. Hold the knife or rasp in a ready position for when you discover spots that need work.

Clamp the knife into the screw vise with the handle up. Cut out some strips of sandpaper to widths of 3 cm (1¼ inch). Holding the handle up, begin with a piece of coarse sandpaper. Wrap it around the back of the handle, then pull it back and forth while moving it up and down along the handle (Fig. 26). Keep a keen

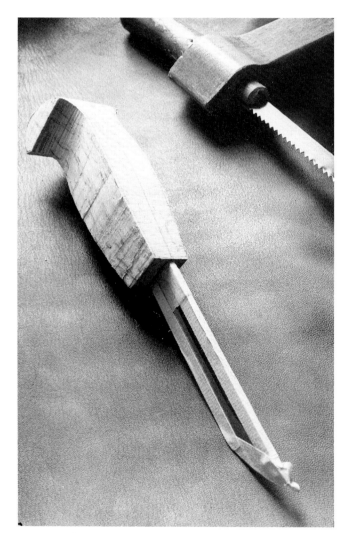

Fig. 22 *The sides of the handle have been sawed out*

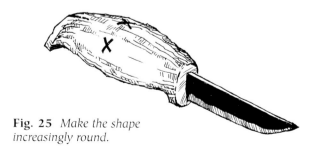

Fig. 25 *Make the shape increasingly round.*

Fig. 26 *Pull sandpaper back and forth across the handle.*

Fig. 27 *Sand by hand, using small pieces of sandpaper.*

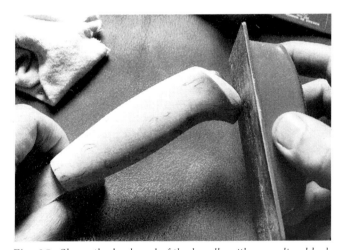

Fig. 28 *Shape the back end of the handle with a sanding block.*

eye on what is happening and have a bright light pointed toward the knife. Go down in coarseness of sandpaper as you go along until you can take out the knife and sand it by hand. Then go down another level of coarseness. Sand by hand, using small pieces of sandpaper, just 3 x 3 cm (1¼ x 1¼ inches), in order to achieve a fine finish (Fig. 27). Change sandpaper coarseness often. Observe the handle carefully over and over again. Hold it lengthwise and crosswise against the light. Do not quit until every indentation, no matter how small, is gone. See also Fig. 28.

Hard-to-remove scratches will occur if you use too much pressure when using coarser sandpaper. Carelessness will cause the worst parts of the surface

treatment to be exposed. Put your patience to the test, and you will have a knife with a finish you have always dreamed of.

FINISHING THE WOODEN HANDLE

There are several different methods that can be used for finishing a wooden handle. We will concentrate on the most common of them, the linseed-oil treatment.

If you began to use your knife as soon as you have finished sanding, it will become a dirty wooden stick in no time. It will be grasped thousands of times, perhaps for an entire lifetime or longer. It will be subject to rain, snow, wind, hand sweat, fish guts, and much more. So it really needs as good a surface treatment as possible in order to endure all these challenges unscathed.

A long time ago, wooden objects were painted with pine tar. Then came linseed oil, which resulted in surfaces that were very tolerant of moisture and very durable. With time, new finishing materials were developed; when common varnish was introduced, it quickly replaced linseed oil. Varnish dried more quickly than linseed oil and gave the shiny, slightly yellowish surface that we all recognize. Varnish is still a pretty good alternative to finishing. It penetrates the wood somewhat, it tolerates moisture, and it is very durable. Who doesn't remember what an unbelievable amount of punishment varnished wood floors could withstand? Thus, if you want a very smooth handle, you may want to varnish it.

A number of knifemakers today treat their knives with semigloss, clear plastic lacquer. Some may see it as a shortcut to the semigloss surface that a linseed oil treatment can give. I suspect that they are deceiving themselves somewhat. It is hard for a beginner to achieve a neat finish with lacquer. It can take years to become an expert in this technique. Holding it to the light, you will discover all the mistakes: a coating that is too thick or too thin, ridges, wrinkles, and empty spots. The plastic lacquer covers like a dead coat on the living wood. Certainly the surface is protected for a while, but there will soon be areas where impurities have penetrated the surface, causing the knife handle to get dirty. And these areas grow. There is only one thing to do when this happens: Rub off the lacquer down to the wood surface and do it all over again. Attempting to "patch" doesn't pay; The surface becomes a patchwork quilt of various lacquer layers. I have also noticed that plastic lacquer does not seem to resist grease very well. Somehow the grease is able to go through the lacquer surface and into the wood.

LINSEED OIL

Linseed oil seeps down into the wood and forms a protective wall against damage. The oil oxidizes in air to form something called *linoxyn*, a hard substance that protects from the inside. Because linoxyn lies deep, you always put your hand on the smooth, well-polished wood surface, which becomes more beautiful with age. Linseed oil does not change the natural aging of the wood.

Don't worry if, contrary to expectations, you don't like the smell of the oil. Within a few weeks, the oil hardens to linoxyn, which has a negligible smell. Also, linoxyn is tasteless, a quality that is important if you happen to use the wrong oil on a cutting board. Only if it is boiled or is left in warm water for a long time does it begin to have a taste.

I prefer linseed oil for several reasons. Knives are often made of curly grained wood (from various types of trees), wavy grained wood, or knotty growths of birch wood—that is, wood in which the best look is drawn out if it gets a moisturizing finish. I have frequently seen factory-made knives made with a lacquer surface that chokes all the best parts of the curly grained wood, making it look as if it was made of synthetic material instead. Also, it is easy for a beginner to succeed with linseed oil, as long as the preparatory work is done carefully. In addition, it is easier to tidy up an oiled knife.

The disadvantage of using oil is that it has a relatively long drying time compared to other materials. It takes time and a little patience to get a beautiful finish. But I definitely believe that it will pay in the long run. Also, linseed oil is a pure, natural product, just like turpentine.

To finish with linseed oil, moisten a piece of cloth in warm water and wipe all the wood surfaces (Fig. 29). Using your pointer finger works well. Moisten only lightly. Put the knife aside to dry for a day. To speed up the process and get a better effect, quickly dry the wood with a hair dryer.

Repeat this procedure at least three times, preferably more. Those with the greatest patience will get the best results. Every time you dry the moistened wood surface, the uppermost fibers rise to the surface. Then take steel wool and carefully polish the surface (Fig. 30). Do not push too hard, or the fibers will lie down. Pay attention to the knife during this phase, since it is very sensitive to dirt. Every time you repeat the process, you reduce the number of residue fibers

Moisten the handle for wood cleaning, then polish it with steel wool in various degrees of coarseness.

Fig. 29

Fig. 30

Brush the handle in the longitudinal direction, then oil it.

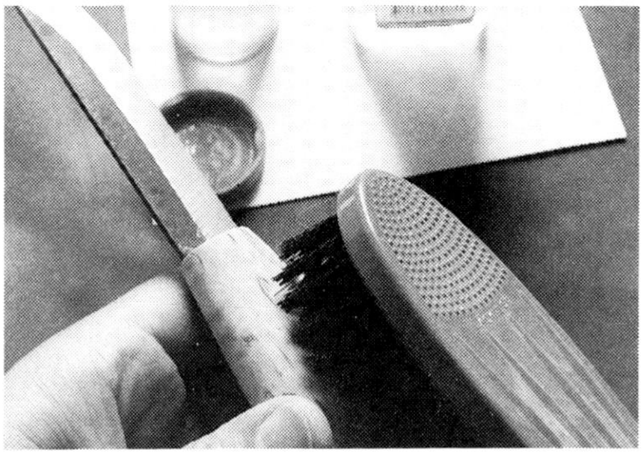

Fig. 31

Fig. 32

that are ground off, and soon you will have a hard, even surface. This treatment is especially important for knives that will come into contact with water.

Once you have brushed off the wood surface (Fig. 31), apply the oil. Mix equal parts of boiled linseed oil and gum turpentine, and shake together. The mixture easily penetrates below the surface. I have tried several fattier mixtures (70 percent oil, 30 percent turpentine, for example). My experience is that, in the fattier mixtures, the majority of the oil remains on top of the polished surface. The pores seem to be too small to allow the mixture to penetrate. You will not capture the beautiful nuances in the wood if the oil does not penetrate deeply enough.

Take a piece of cloth and coat the handle (Fig. 32). Stroke the handle a lot to allow the oil to seep into the surface. Repeat as soon as the surface dries again. Continue this procedure until the wood is saturated. Depending on the wood, this process can take

anywhere from an hour up to a day.

If this seems too time-consuming, try another method. Find an oblong glass jar with a lid and wash it out. I use a pickle jar. The jar must be tall enough so that more than the entire handle fits down into it. Make your linseed oil mixture and fill the jar almost to the top. Then make a slit in the middle of the lid so that knife tips of various shapes can poke through. Then sink the whole handle down into the oil, put the lid over the tip of the knife, and screw it shut. Tape any openings that remain. Let the knife sit, absorbing the oil, for a couple of days. Keep checking the handle until it reaches the desired color.

If the linseed oil has not completely penetrated the wood surface after a couple of hours, you must dry the surface carefully. If it is allowed to stay longer, the oil will form a skin and harden, and, in the worst cases, can be impossible to get it off. No oil should remain on the surface when you put the knife away to dry. Let the knife sit at least four days, preferably a week, until the oil has hardened into linoxyn. During that time, do not apply any more oil to it.

Do not think that you can only use boiled linseed oil. Raw linseed oil also works well. The raw oil penetrates into the wood surface more easily and does not turn yellow. Its biggest disadvantage is it requires a long drying time. Count on it taking nearly six months to completely dry! Thus, the drying time will determine whether you choose boiled or raw linseed oil.

When the weeks of hardening have passed, polish the surface of the handle with steel wool (3/0) that has been dunked in linseed oil. Use plenty of oil on both the handle and in the steel wool and rub in the direction of the wood's fiber. Rub really well! Then carefully dry the surface with paper or rags. All the oil and dust must be removed. Then allow the surface to dry again as above.

You can rub in the oil the first time you coat the wood, but remember the residue from the oil can penetrate into the pores and discolor the wood.

After the oil hardens (a week), then dries, brush the surface, first with a hard brush, then with a softer brush, in the direction of wood's fiber. Finally, dry the knife lightly with paper.

NOTE: The knife must be separate from the sheath during hardening. Otherwise, the leather will suck the oil out of the wood and you will have to start all over. Repeat the wet polishing with fine steel wool at this point and again during the following years. The handle will become more beautiful with time.

TAR

Why not treat your new knife in the same ancient manner as oak is treated—with pine tar? Tar has primarily been used outside of the home for tar paper on houses and for bridges and boats, but it works fine on things inside the home as well. The handle of the knife will be beautiful, with a warm, reddish-brown color. It will be unsusceptible to moisture and water, and emit a wonderful smell.

Heat the tar until it becomes a very thin liquid, rub it on your handle, then dry it off with a rag. If the tar is too thick, it can be thinned with French turpentine—not petroleum spirits! Thick tar can also be mixed with boiled linseed oil. Take one part of each and thin it with turpentine.

WAXING

To bring out that wonderful, old-fashioned luster in your knife that you may not have succeeded in bringing out otherwise, use wax! The wax you need to use in knifemaking is called *PIMA-wax* and is actually a mixture of various types of wax that are melted together. In all kinds of wood and in horn, wax gives a semigloss finish, without all the disadvantages of lacquer. The surface gets hard and repels moisture and water, but it still gives the same slip-free grip that a pure-oil treatment gives. That the handle still smells of linseed oil and turpentine after the wax treatment is an advantage, too. But the biggest advantage is the beautiful surface that the wax provides. I believe few other methods can compete in this respect. The colors are deepened and the wood grain is brought out.

Wax can be used in two ways. If you are using hard wax, melt a small piece of wax in a vessel. When the wax is liquid, apply it to the handle with a paintbrush or rag. I prefer to use small, hard artist's paintbrushes. The wax has to be rubbed over the surface at once, little by little. You only have a couple of seconds before it gets hard again! (Scrape off any "ridges" that may appear in the wax with a nail.) Then you have to polish immediately, and you must apply the polish well! A knife takes quite a long time to finish by this method, but it results in the thickest protective surface possible.

If you are using wax paste, melt a small amount of wax as you would for hard wax; but dilute the liquid wax with two parts of gum turpentine. Let the paste cool before you use it. Then apply the paste with a cotton rag, polishing as above.

MIXED-MATERIAL HANDLES

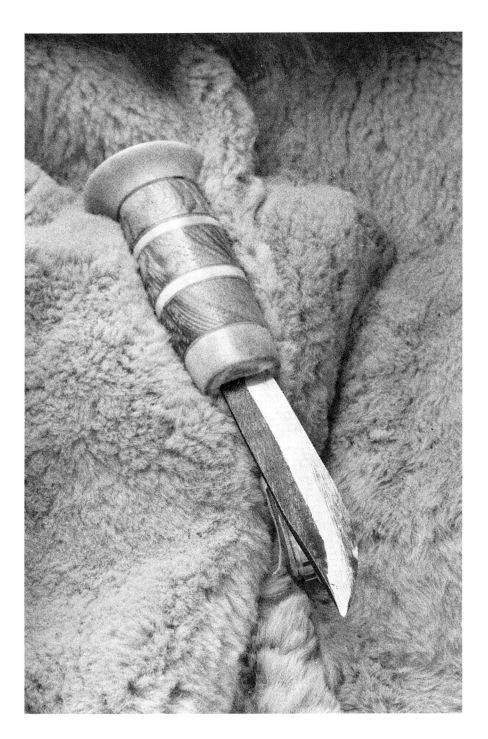

This knife is made of mixed materials and is based on the Sami knife. The handle is made of reindeer antler, pine-root pieces, and birch bark. The knife has a hand-forged carbonized steel blade. Make sure the handle is relatively straight in order to fit a knife sheath made of Sami knife leather.

I have a feeling that, in many respects, the image many aspiring knifemakers have of their ideal knife is one that resembles the classic Sami knife. Anyone with an eye for beauty can't avoid being fascinated by a genuine Sami knife. Its aesthetic value is enhanced by the knowledge that these knives are superbly useable and have been tried and tested in daily work for hundreds of years. Every feature of this knife has shown its worth and any aspect of the knife that was not up to standard has been redesigned. Sami knives are, therefore, completely suited to outdoor life and outdoor work. They have come from nature itself—a harsh and unpredictable nature. Today, a Sami knife costs quite a bit, and I think they are worth every penny. These knives embody a unique cultural inheritance and are often made by people who have been trained in the craft since childhood.

I advise against the rest of us trying to make Sami knives exactly, because I believe that only the Sami can make genuine Sami knives. We do not have their cultural inheritance, and few knifemakers can achieve the same feeling for style, skill, and sensitivity, using other methods. But we can use their experience in our own knives for beautiful, strong knives that we can trust.

But why not use Sami knives as sources of inspiration for our own knives? If we use the best materials, perhaps the Sami will someday cast a dreamy glance on our knives.

I call this type of knife, or a utilitarian knife of the norland type, the *mixed knife*. (See page 88 for a color photograph of a mixed knife.) These handles can be made a number of ways, from handles that are made almost completely of antlers to handles made of layered pieces of wood, horn, leather, birch bark, or metal to handles made of wood or leather segments. You can mix pieces of horn, wood, leather, or birch bark almost any way you like. But in general, limitations make the master. If you attempt to make a handle with the largest possible number of various materials, perhaps it will be a creation even you won't want to carry!

We will begin with a handle that is very easy to make. You will need pieces of curly grained wood, horn, and birch bark (Fig. 1). (A few pieces of aluminum plate may also be needed.) As with the previous knife, select a blade that is about 80 mm (about 3¼ inches) long. The knife tang should be about 110 mm (about 4 to 4½ inches) long. In order not to make the handle too narrow, you must attempt to get the thickest possible horn.

The handle should be very straight if you are thinking of using Sami knife leather in the sheath. Sami knife leather hardly stretches at all. You will not be able to pull a handle that is too oval out of the sheath.

Fig. 1 *Materials for the Sami handle*

SKETCHING AND PREPARING THE HANDLE

Begin by sketching the handle you want on a piece of greaseproof paper. A handle of horn is very durable, but nothing prevents you from beginning with pieces of curly grained wood instead. If you use horn, make sure the end pieces are as free of marrow as possible. The less marrow, the stronger the knife. When you rivet, remember that the handle should be narrowest at the point where it is closest to the blade. Do not make the handle too oval—that is, with a big "stomach" in the middle. Then it will be hard to make a functional sheath. I imagined my handle to be like the one in Fig. 2. Remember to wrap the blade with masking tape.

Begin by sawing out the pieces you will need from the materials you have gathered. Two 1.5-cm

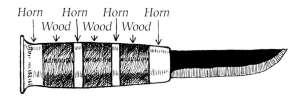

Fig. 2

(½-inch) pieces of horn are needed (Fig. 3). The back curved piece should be made from the rosenkrans (see page 12). Estimate that each one will be sawed to about 1.7 cm (⅝ inch) in length. The ends must be evened out, which takes off a couple of millimeters (¹⁄₁₆ inch). Three 2 cm (¾ inch) pieces of wood are also needed. They should be first sawed to 2.2 cm (⅞ inch), then evened out to 2 cm (¾ inch). Saw out

two thin slices of horn, which will ultimately be .5 cm (¼ inch) thick each. Each piece of horn should be about 4.5 x 4.5 cm (1¾ x 1¾ inches). Finally, six pieces of birch bark are needed, each also measuring about 4.5 x 4.5 cm (1¾ x 1¾ inches).

Attach a coarse piece of sandpaper to your workbench with a small clamp. You can also fasten the paper to a flat piece of board with a tack on the bottom. The end surfaces of the horn and the pieces of wood must now be sanded completely flat (Fig. 4). Hold each piece from the very bottom; your fingers should almost touch the sandpaper. This is to prevent the end pieces from "rolling." Sand two or three times in one direction, turn the piece 45°, and repeat. Continue for one revolution. This prevents the end surfaces from becoming sanded unevenly. Lift each piece up to the light and make sure that no notches or pits remain, particularly near the outer edges. It is equally important for the pieces to be of the same thickness. Do not do shoddy work here! It helps to use a caliper and move it around all sides. It is essential that the pieces fit together precisely.

Fig. 3 *Saw the pieces of horn.*

Fig. 4 *Sand the pieces flat, keeping them parallel to the sandpaper.*

38

MOUNTING THE HANDLE

Now that the pieces are ready, it is time to begin putting them together. Begin with the pieces of horn that are to be placed at the bottom of the knife tang, or the piece closest to the blade. Draw a straight line in the middle of the end surfaces of each piece of horn. Measure how wide the tang is at the point where the piece is going to fit and transfer the measurement to the middle of the straight line.

Using a high-speed, steel drill bit that is as thick as the tang, drill two outer holes inside your markings. Do your best to drill straight down. Then saw off the piece in the middle (between the holes) with a fret saw or a jigsaw fitted with a hacksaw blade. If the hole is right, you should be able to press the piece down over the tang; it should be a stiff fit. Check the fit of the blade.

Fig. 6 *Handle pieces are threaded onto the tang, then riveted.*

that allow for the harder material's movements. They are also beautiful, and, when moist, they swell a little and prevent the knife from becoming slippery. In addition, they camouflage any unevenness.

Finally, make a rectangular hole in the middle of the first piece of wood to fit exactly on the tang, which is narrower at this point. All three finished pieces must very slowly be pushed down onto the tang and into the correct position (Fig. 5).

Mix enough epoxy glue for three pieces. Put a thin layer of glue on every surface that comes into contact with another surface. Thread the large piece of horn, the piece of birch bark, and the piece of wood, in this order. Then take a piece of pipe (which is protected on the bottom with leather) or a round piece of wood with a hole drilled in the longitudinal direction, and push or tap the pieces gently into place. (NOTE: No glue is applied to the surfaces that do not touch other pieces.) Twist and turn the glued sections under bright light, and check that the pieces pack against each other exactly. Correct if necessary. Then put aside your work for a day and let the glue harden.

Because they are not as broad, we can now begin to mount the following pieces (in this order): birch bark, piece of horn, birch bark, piece of wood. Proceed as before (see previous paragraph). Measure the tang width exactly where each piece will sit (Fig. 6). Then begin to make rectangular holes in each piece. Don't do a shoddy job here, even though the

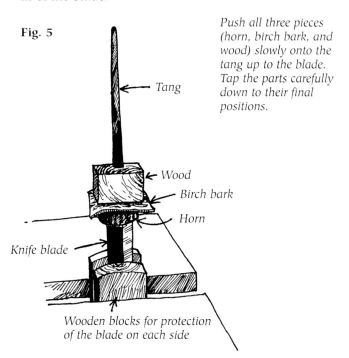

Fig. 5

Push all three pieces (horn, birch bark, and wood) slowly onto the tang up to the blade. Tap the parts carefully down to their final positions.

Tang

Wood

Birch bark

Horn

Knife blade

Wooden blocks for protection of the blade on each side

Next, take a piece of birch bark, peel off all the white material, and make a rectangular hole in the middle of it, using a sharp knife. The pieces of birch bark have an important function. They are buffers

Fig. 7 *The last six pieces, from the middle to the rosenkrans*

A QUICK KNIFE-MOUNTING METHOD

Saw out a groove in a piece of wood that is as thick as the blade of the knife. The groove must be a little wider and longer than the dimensions of the blade. Make all the pieces for the handle and lay them out on a table in front of you in the proper order. Spread epoxy glue on the surface of all the pieces that will touch each other, and mount all of them. Then press

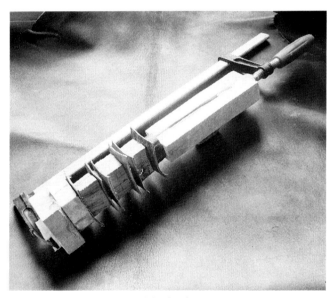

Fig. 8 *Quick mounting of the knife*

work would go much faster if you only drill one hole in them. Next, put a thin layer of epoxy glue on all the surfaces that come into contact with each other. Then push down each piece into place with the pipe piece as before. Examine in bright light. Do not allow any gaps between the parts.

Put it aside again to allow the glue to dry. If you do this in the morning, you can continue in the evening with the last pieces: birch bark, narrow horn piece, birch bark, piece of wood, birch bark, large piece of horn (Fig. 7). You will use the same process as before, with one difference. For the large piece on the end of the handle, simply drill a regular hole in the middle. The hole should be so small that you have to hit the piece to get it in place. Let the handle harden for a day.

If the tang sticks out too far, saw it with a hacksaw and even it out until about 1 mm (1/32 inch) sticks out beyond the end piece. If you are able to find a piece of rosenkrans for the end of the handle, you can rivet the knife tang directly against it. For a regular piece of horn, I suggest you rivet with a rivet washer between instead. Otherwise, the knife will start to have play in its parts when the rivet head sinks into the loose marrow.

the handle together, using a piece of wood with a groove. Also, place a small piece of wood behind the end piece for protection. Press all of it together with a bar-clamp (Fig. 8).

This method saves a lot of time, since there is only one gluing step and one hardening period. The disadvantage of using this method is that, if the pieces don't fit together perfectly and there are gaps, there is high risk of having problems (in respect to both the beauty and durability of the knife) in certain places if the clamp is not perfectly centered.

Fig. 9 *Roughly shape the handle with a rasp.*

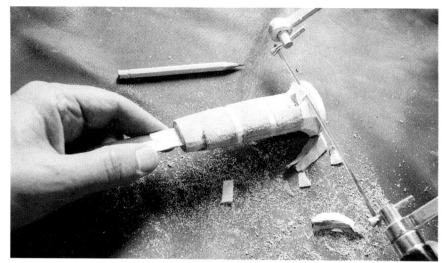

Fig. 11 *Shaping the end*

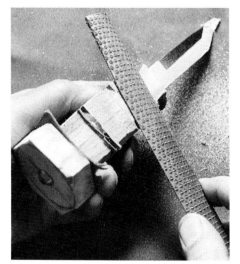

Fig. 10 *Saw or rasp the top of the knife.*

Fig. 12 *A roughly shaped handle*

SHAPING THE HANDLE

Now we have come to the best part—shaping the handle. First, mark the shape of the handle on your work. Using a jigsaw equipped with a blade for sawing metal, saw along the contours. First remove the pieces from the top and the bottom of the handle, then saw the side pieces. Rasp and saw the handle to an increasingly round shape as described for the wooden handle on page 30 (see Figs. 9 through 12 above).

Then move on to working with sandpaper. Remember that wood is much softer than horn, so be particularly careful with the joints between wood and horn.

Begin as with the wooden handle, using coarse sandpaper, working your way down to very fine sandpaper (Fig. 13); You may also need a half-round file and a sanding block for the edges (Figs. 14 and 15). Scratches from coarse sandpaper have a much greater tendency to remain in horn than in wood, so do not press too hard when using the coarse paper

Fig. 13 *Shape the handle with sandpaper.*

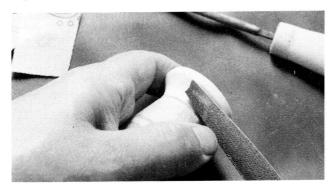

Fig. 14 *Refine the curved part of the back end with a half-round file.*

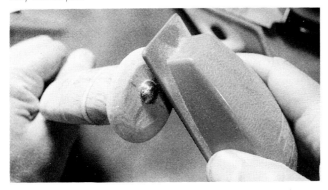

Fig. 15 *Shape and smooth the top of the back end with a sanding block.*

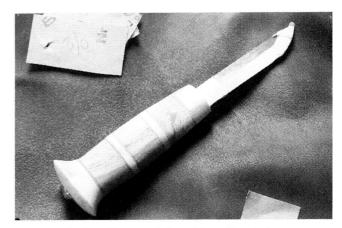

Fig. 16 *The handle is sanded, and is waiting to be treated with oil.*

and be prepared to spend more time polishing the horn. Polish several times as described on page 32, then do the final polishing with steel wool.

FINISHING

The last step is oiling the handle with the same mixture as was used on the wooden handle (see page 32). This gives the horn a wonderful luster. However, do not keep the horn in oil as long as you do with wood or an ugly, yellowish discoloration can result. Lacquer them if you wish with a plastic lacquer, but use only a few thin layers.

I do not discuss how to engrave in horn in this book. It is not something that can be learned in a short time. This is where most non-Sami knifemakers who want to make a Sami knife fail. The art must be practiced almost from childhood. Engraving also requires artistic ability, talent, and daily practice in order to succeed. The technique is tricky to learn and get used to. But if you must try, practice on scrap pieces—never on a finished knife. You can also refer to engraving instructions in a book on Sami woodworking.

Do not be surprised if you discover that it is possible to bend your new knife handle in various directions. This is due to the soft leather layers in the knife. These will harden with time as the knife settles.

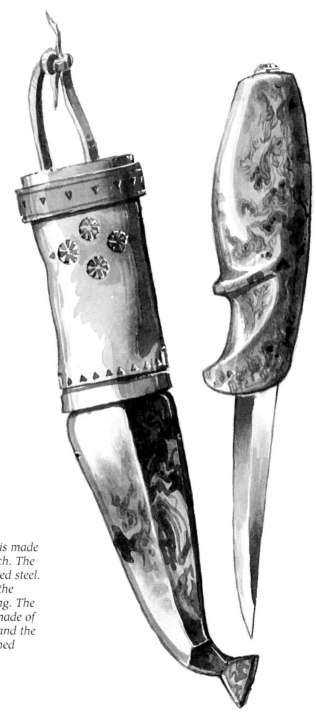

Carving Knife. This handle is made entirely of curly grained birch. The blade is laminated carbonized steel. The handle is shaped to fit the hand perfectly during carving. The lower part of the sheath is made of curly grained birch as well and the upper part of vegetable-tanned leather.

LEATHER OR BIRCH BARK HANDLES

A knife with a birch bark handle. The handle, inspired by a traditional design, is soft, warm, and easy to hold.

If you have lots of scrap pieces of thick leather or birch bark, you can make a knife handle with these materials. Scrap pieces of strong, vegetable-tanned leather can also be purchased and are inexpensive. Birch bark may be obtained commercially if you are unable to find it in nearby woodlands. Leather and birch bark, however, do not work as the beginning or end layers of the handle. Something

harder is necessary. Pieces of horn are excellent for this purpose, as is hard wood and brass plates that are at least 2 mm (about 1/16 inch) thick. See page 89 for a color photograph of a knife with a birch bark handle.

First, prepare the birch bark (Fig, 1), then cut out squares of birch bark or leather to a suitable size (Fig. 2). You will need quite a few. In the middle of each piece, make a hole for the tang of the knife. Many recommend punching tongs or a hollow punch, but I think these tools are too rough. In thicker birch bark, for example, every piece you hit with a hollow punch or drill with a thick drill bit splits. I drill two holes with a small drill bit that is the thickness of the tang (Fig. 3), then turn these holes into one rectangular hole with a sharp knife (Fig. 4). It takes a little longer, but you get whole pieces. The leather is equally thick, but you can smooth out the surfaces that touch the birch bark with a rasp, or peel off the outer layer with a knife.

Next, make a rectangular hole shaped like the tang in the stop piece. Then stack the leather or pieces of birch bark (Figs. 5 and 6). Use epoxy glue to glue between each piece. I suggest that you don't glue more than five to ten pieces at a time, partly because the glue will not be able to harden, and also because you need complete control over the fit. To speed up the process, longer strips of leather can be cut. Glue several strips together with epoxy glue so that you get more bundles. Apply pressure! After drying, cut the bundles into suitable lengths (Fig. 7). Make holes through each stack as explained above. Thread the tang and glue these larger pieces together. Then press the pieces together carefully.

When you have reached far enough up, add the other stop piece. Measure so as to allow only a few millimeters (about $\frac{1}{16}$ inch) to stick up over the rivet

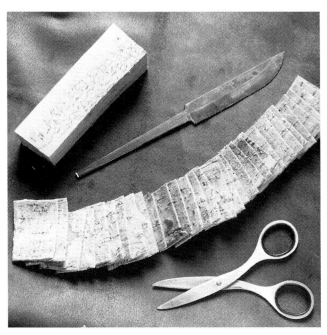

Fig. 2 *Cut-out pieces of birch bark, the block for the end pieces, and the knife blade*

Fig. 1 *Peel off the white coating on the birch bark.*

Fig. 3 *Drill the holes for the tang.*

Fig. 4 *Connect the drill holes into a rectangular shape, using a knife or chisel.*

45

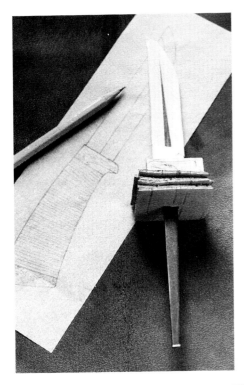

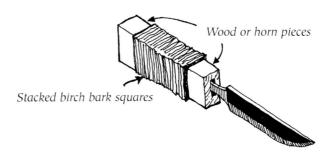

Stacked birch bark squares   Wood or horn pieces

Fig. 6 *Knife with a birch bark or leather handle*

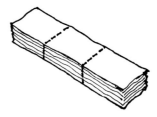

Fig. 5 *The upper end pieces and the first batch of birch bark squares glued together*

Fig. 7 *Glue together longer strips in bundles then divide*

Fig. 8 *Once the handle has been glued together, put it in a bar-clamp.*

washer. At this point, it is a matter of having enough pressure to keep the whole thing together. There are two methods. You can tap the upper part of the tang a little with a thread tap. These are not cheap, so see if you can borrow or rent one from a hardware dealer for a single job. Then take an appropriate size castle nut and screw it on until the handle doesn't move.

Otherwise, you can use a large rivet washer to rivet the tang of the knife. What remains to be done, after a few days of drying (Fig. 8), is to shape the

handle with a knife, rasp, file, and sandpaper (see Figs. 9 through 12).

Leather and particularly birch bark handles provide a better grip than other materials. You will especially notice the difference when it is wet outside. They are warm and beautiful in the cold and, at the same time, if you haven't lacquered them, they absorb hand sweat on warm days. You may think that these handles will be loose or flimsy, but, with the proper finishing, the surfaces become as hard as

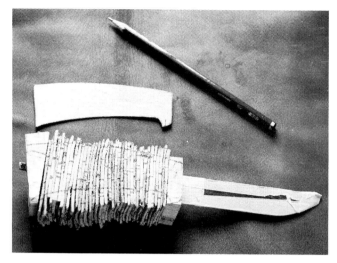

Fig. 9 *Trace a cardboard model on the side of the handle.*

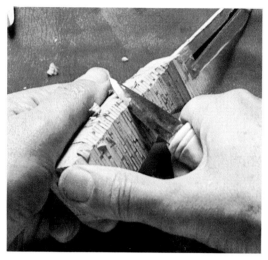

Fig. 11 *Roughly shape with a carving knife.*

Fig. 10 *Saw out the handle.*

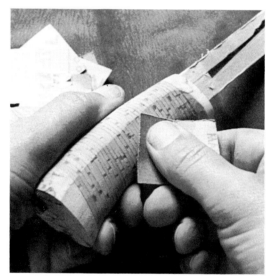

Fig. 12 *Sand the handle with sandpaper of various grades of coarseness.*

if they were made of wood.

Commercially made knives of leather or birch bark are often coated with clear lacquer, which decreases the effectiveness of the grip. But you can sand these handles with fine sandpaper until the lacquer is gone. Polish leather handles with fine steel wool that has been dipped in leather grease, then sand the handle. Polish handles made of birch bark with steel wool dipped in a linseed oil/gum turpentine mixture.

Let the knife sit a few days, then polish it again, as described above. Repeat this process five to ten times. Remember to continue to grease the handle well two or three times a year. If you do this, you will not be stuck with a soft, flimsy handle that smells bad. The result will be a knife in the ancient tradition. I think there are too few knives made from these wonderful materials today.

SIMPLE KNIVES

I will conclude my discussion of knifemaking basics with a couple simple handles. The first is among the easiest to make. But don't think this means that the knife will be ugly or a bad tool! You will get a completely useful knife in a very short time. And with some imagination and a little creative zeal, it can become a beautiful tool that is tailored to your needs. However, you should remember that these models can't withstand the hardest stress.

SIMPLE KNIFE WITH A WOODEN HANDLE

This method involves simply nailing a nail-shaped knife tang into a piece of wood, then shaping the piece of wood into a handle.

Use a knife blade of carbonized steel, approximately 7 to 8 cm (about 2¾ to 3¼ inches) long, that is neither too hard nor very expensive. Secure the blade in a vise or on a tabletop with a clamp. Do not forget to put protective tape on the blade first.

Cut off the knife tang with a hacksaw to a length of about 6 to 7 cm (2¼ to 2¾ inches). Shape the tang so that it becomes the same thickness from the tip all the way to the blade, 7 to 10 mm (about ⅜ inch) is sufficient (Fig. 1). Then file down the groove (the outwardly curving part of the tang that is closest to the blade) so that you get a right angle (Fig. 2). If the groove is allowed to remain, there is a great risk that it will act like a wedge and split the handle material (the piece of wood) when you hit the last section into place.

Next, file down the edges of the tang so that it forms a knifelike edge on the upper and lower side (Fig. 3). File the tip on the tang to a point, somewhat like a nail (refer to Fig. 3 for the approximate measurements and appearance). These details take quite a while to complete. Therefore, it may be a good idea to divide this job over two days to avoid getting tired.

When choosing fresh wood for the handle, you should remember that most domestic types of wood split in the core when they dry. Therefore, I advise using juniper wood. Juniper is one of the few kinds of wood that seldom splits when drying. It is strong and tough, but still easy to cut when fresh. In addition, it emits a wonderful smell while it is being worked. Juniper is found almost everywhere, but don't forget to get permission before you cut any.

Where there is a larger selection of wood, look for ash, beech, and oak. I usually use ash brushwood that is cut down along roads every year. It is thick enough for the handle of a knife and a piece of a branch will usually work for a single knife.

Saw off a piece of wood that is a little longer

than the width of your hand. Secure the blade in a vise, with the tip of the tang pointing upwards and the tip of the blade resting against a thick piece of wood (Fig. 4, left). Picture the tang in the middle of the core of the handle material, then split the handle carefully with an ax or similar tool. Carefully make sure that the handle and blade are aligned with each other! To keep the blade from twisting inside the handle, you can also bevel the blunt edges of the blade (Fig. 4, right). But only sharpen one side of these edges, enough to make the blade stick. Otherwise, there is a risk of splitting the handle.

Next, shape your handle with a knife, rasp, file, and sandpaper (Fig. 5). Coat the ends of the wood with a good layer of wood cement. This lengthens the drying time, thereby reducing the risk of splitting (which is caused by drying). Grease the finished knife with boiled linseed oil or paraffin oil.

SIMPLE KNIFE WITH A SHORT WOODEN HANDLE

There are several reasons why this knife is considerably easier to make than the previous knives I have

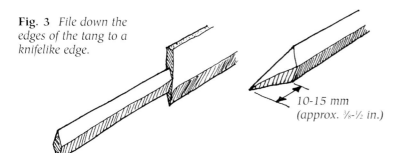

Fig. 1
Cross-cut the knife tang to approximately 7 cm (2¾ in.) in length.

6-7 cm (2¼-2¾ in.)

Shape the tang so that it is all one width.

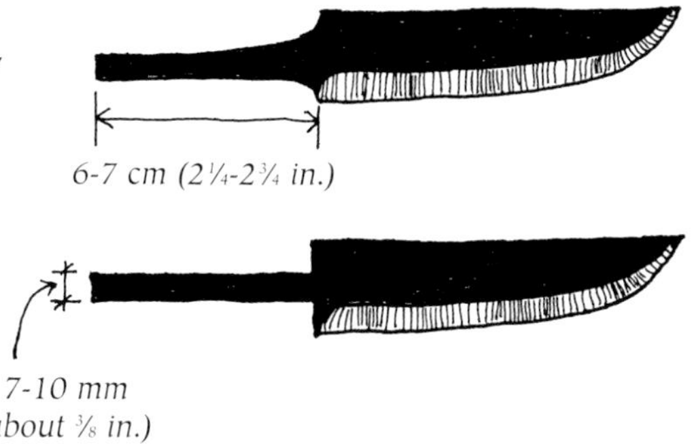

7-10 mm (about ⅛ in.)

Right angles.

Fig. 2 *File down the groove to get a right angle.*

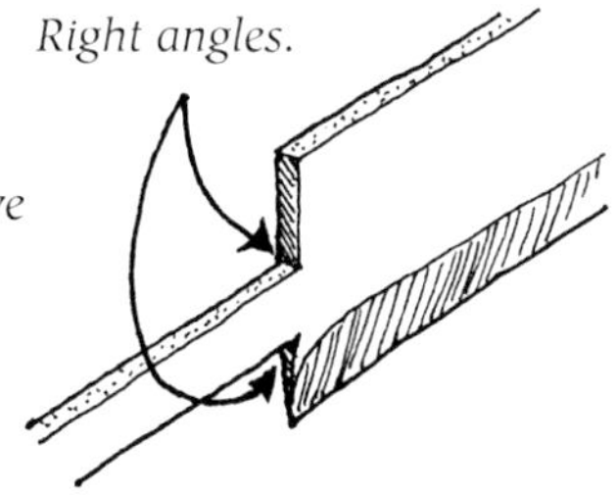

Fig. 3 *File down the edges of the tang to a knifelike edge.*

10-15 mm (approx. ⅛-½ in.)

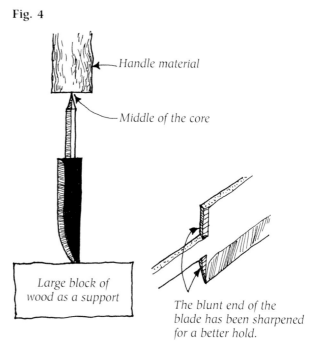

Fig. 4

Handle material

Middle of the core

Large block of wood as a support

The blunt end of the blade has been sharpened for a better hold.

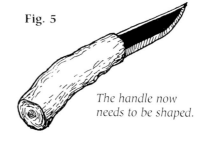

Fig. 5

The handle now needs to be shaped.

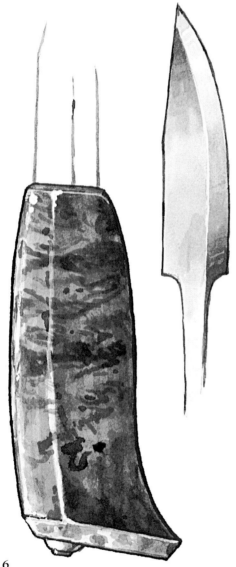

Fig. 6

discussed. The handle is short and easy to drill straight through. The handle is easier to shape, and the back end is completely straight, which makes the knife tang easy to rivet.

Purchase a knife blade of carbonized steel at a well-stocked hardware dealer. You can also order one from a mail-order supplier. The blade should not exceed 8 to 9 cm (about 3 to 3½ inches). Preferably, it should be shorter, since the knife will be disproportional otherwise.

My handle is drawn to full scale (Fig. 6). You will need to sketch your own pattern, but preferably do not make the handle any longer than mine. Sketch the handle pattern on paper. Hold the back side and the paper against a window so you can see through. Cut out along the contours of the handle. Put your pattern on the wood you are using for the handle and draw along the edges onto the wood. Darken the lines so they are visible. Saw out the handle, leaving a good margin around the edges.

Put the tang of the knife blade flush against the side of the piece of wood (Fig. 7). The back end of the knife blade must lie edge to edge against the front end of the piece of wood. Trace the knife tang. Now you know how large the hole in the handle needs to be.

Draw a vertical line in the middle of the front end of the handle (Fig. 8). This is where the blade will enter the handle. Draw a line on the top side of the piece of handle as well. Draw a line down the middle of the back end of the handle. The tang will come out in the center of this line.

Measure the thickness of the blade. On the front end of the handle piece, draw the rectangular hole were the tang is to enter (Fig. 9). Now drill two holes about 2 to 3 cm (¾ to 1¼ inches) into the wood, inside the upper and lower ends of the hole. The drill bit must be as thick as the knife blade. Rotate the piece of wood; then, using a thicker drill bit (as wide as the tang), drill a hole from the back so that the holes meet. Use tape to mark the drill bit so that you don't drill too far in from the back! Saw (with a fret saw, for example) and file a rectangular hole on the front end. Try to push the tang into the hole occasionally. File the hole until you can push almost the entire tang into the handle. Only a few centimeters (about ¾ inch) of the tang should remain outside. Remove the blade.

Secure the blade in a vise, using a small piece of wood or leather to protect the blade. Mix a batch of epoxy glue and fill the hole. Thread on the piece of handle and tap it carefully into place all the way up the blade. Tap with a wooden or rubber mallet. (If you do not have a vise, rest the tip of the knife against a piece of thick wood and follow the above procedure. However, there is a risk that the tip may become damaged!)

NOTE: The knife tang should not stick out more than 5 mm (¹¹⁄₆₄ inch) from the back (Fig. 10). If it does, saw it off with a hacksaw. Measure carefully. Take a rivet washer and file a hole in it that fits the back tip of the tang exactly.

When you have tapped the handle piece into place, put on the finished rivet washer at the back and tap on the end of the tang with a ball peen hammer until it spreads out and sits firmly against the washer (see Fig. 10). You have to rivet quickly before the glue hardens (about five minutes), so have everything ready ahead of time. Let it dry about a day before you continue.

Shape the handle with a knife or rasp, a file, and sandpaper. When you have finished sanding (using sandpaper with several levels of coarseness), wet a small piece of cotton cloth and moisten the wood surface. Dry immediately with a hair dryer. Polish the wood that rises to the surface with fine steel wool. Repeat at least twice.

Drown the knife in a mixture of 70 percent boiled linseed oil and 30 percent gum (spirits of) turpentine. Continue until the surface can't take any more!

Now you need to hone the blade if it hasn't already been honed. Let the oil harden for at least a week before you use your knife.

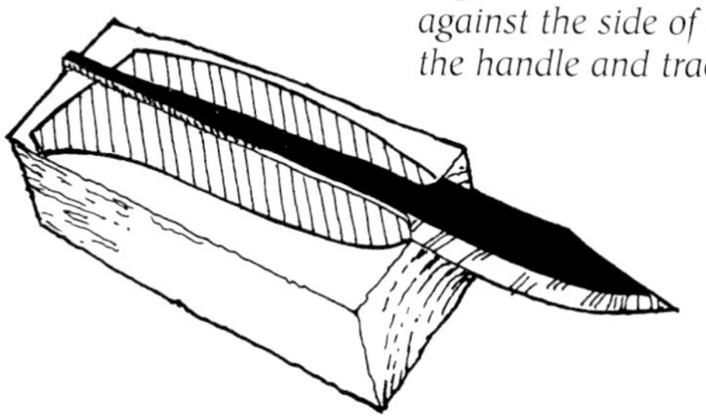

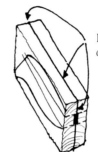

Fig. 7 *Place the knife tang flush against the side of the material for the handle and trace around it.*

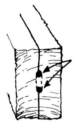

Fig. 8 *Draw the middle lines on the front and back sides.*

Fig. 9 *Drill two holes of the same diameter as the thickness of the blade. Saw and file a hole between them.*

Max. 5 mm (¹¹⁄₆₄ in.) outside.

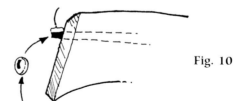

Fig. 10

Rivet washer with a rectangular hole

WEDGED HANDLES

Another fairly simple knifemaking method is to wedge the blade into the handle with wooden wedges. First, measure how thick the knife tang is at the base (next to the blade) and in the middle of the tang (Fig.1). Then drill a hole into the handle material. Make the hole as wide as the tang is in the middle. This hole must be as deep as the entire length of the tang. Then take a drill bit of the diameter of the base of the tang and drill in the same hole again, this time only as deep as half the length of the tang (Fig. 2).

Position the knife tang in the hole. You may need to file the hole a little so that your knife tang fits into the hole. When the tang is pressed into place in the handle, carve two wedges. They must be large enough to be tapped on each side of the blade into the handle (see Fig. 2). Next, fill the hole with epoxy glue and tap the wedges in snugly. When they will not go in any further, cut them off flush with the handle.

LENGTHENING THE TANG

Once in a while, you will have a knife blade in which the tang is not long enough for your hand. Specialty blades vary quite a bit in this respect.

Assume the tang ends approximately where the back of the handle begins. From the side, it should look similar to the drawing (Fig. 3). First, simply rivet the tang, preferably with a rivet washer if there is room. I drill two perpendicular holes about 10 mm (⅜ inch) deep above and below the rivet washer. The holes should be about 5 mm ($^{11}/_{64}$ inch) in diameter. Then glue a round dowel that sticks out about 10 mm (⅜ inch) into each hole. Blacken the tops of the dowels with black lead and press them against the surface of the piece that will be the tip of the handle. The impression should indicate where to drill in 10 mm (⅜ inch) so that the dowel will fit. When the fit is correct, roughly shape the back end, then glue it to the handle with epoxy glue, applying pressure.

This joint is very durable, since there isn't as much pressure at the back end of the handle. The dowels can be purchased, but I make my own from hard woods, such as oak, beech, ash, or curly grained birch. You can add an even longer piece at the back end of the knife. If you finely sand the surfaces to be glued together, you will hardly notice the joint. It is even less noticeable when the end piece is made of the same piece of wood as the handle. One advantage is that the entire back end of the knife is smooth, with no rivet shells or rivet washers to get in the way, and no danger of rust!

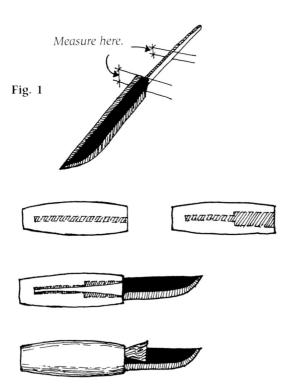

Measure here.

Fig. 1

Fig. 2 *The steps for making a wedged handle*

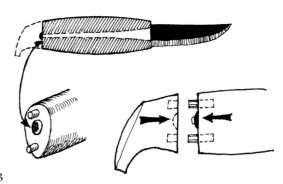

Fig. 3

52

Fig. 4 *Ferrules of various dimensions, and two knives made using ferrules*

FERRULES

A knife *ferrule* is the caplike metal edge that sits at the point where the blade is attached (Fig. 4). The purpose of the ferrule is to strengthen the handle at the point where the blade is attached, so that splitting doesn't occur; the pressure on a knife is the greatest at that point. There are many styles of knife ferrules that can be made of many different materials. The length of the ferrule varies, from under 1 centimeter (⅜ inch) up to about 3 centimeters (1¼ inch). Ferrules are commonly made of brass, but aluminum and other metals are also used.

In order for the ferrule to be effective, there should not be any play between the ferrule and the handle. Many commercially made knives have ferrules, although there is more of a variety among handcrafted knives. Some knifemakers feel knives are "purer" without the ferrule. I seldom use ferrules anymore, because it gives me complete freedom to shape the attachment to the knife however I like. I might want to make a curve instead of the usual straight cut, or even try another shape. I think ferrules lock me too much into the standard knife shapes.

However, a ferrule is useful, because it provides strength. But you must not forget that most ferrule models are quite narrow at the very top. Thus, there isn't much wood or bone for strength. Without the ferrule, I always make the handle thicker at the place where the blade is attached. The equation is as follows: ferrule + frail wood = no ferrule + thicker wood. So the decision to use a ferrule is a matter of appearance.

To mount a ferrule on a knife, the fit must be precise. Since the ferrule is mounted with the blade, it is among the first things you must consider when making a knife. First, center the ferrule in the middle of the opening you made for the knife tang, and trace how much space it requires at the far end of the handle. Measure the height of the ferrule on the handle material. Then work the handle shape with a rasp, file, and sandpaper, using your marks and the ferrule

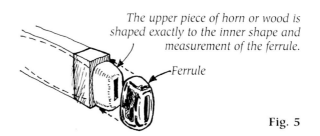

The upper piece of horn or wood is shaped exactly to the inner shape and measurement of the ferrule.

—Ferrule

Fig. 5

as guides. Keep testing the fit (Fig. 5). Twist, press, and adjust until the ferrule sits immobile on the handle. Also, mark the length of the ferrule on the handle so that you will know when the ferrule is all the way on. Glue the inside with epoxy glue and, before it begins to harden, pound the tang into the handle material and rivet it on the back side.

SEWING LEATHER

When you sew leather at the back of a sheath, use *saddler's stitch*. This stitch has a very old tradition, and gives a strong and sure stitch. As mentioned earlier, sinew thread, pitch thread, or waxed linen thread are excellent threads (see page 19). Even if linen thread is waxed, you should pull it through beeswax one more time and wipe off the excess wax. You will need two number 3 saddler's needles; these needles have a rounded tip. For an all-leather sheath, you should have about .5 m (about 1½ feet) of thread. For an upper sheath, you will need about 3 dm (about 12 inches).

First, thread a needle on each end of your piece of thread. To prevent the thread from sliding off the eye of the needle, put the needle back through the middle of the thread (Fig. 1, top). Do this with both needles.

Next, mark where the stitches go. If you have to make an individual sheath for each new knife, you won't be able to mark where each stitch hole will go in advance. If this is the case, wrap the piece of leather around the knife and hold it together, stretching it as much as possible on the back side of the knife. After stretching the leather for an hour, you will see the outline of the knife through the leather—the shape your seam should follow as accurately as possible. If you find it difficult to eyeball the approximate distance between the holes for the stitches, use a pricking wheel (with 4 to 5 mm or ⁵⁄₃₂ to ¹¹⁄₆₄ inch between the tips). Roll it along the area where the stitches will go, a few millimeters (¹⁄₁₆ inch) above the angle that is formed between the back side of the sheath and the leather that sticks up (which you hold on to and stretch). See Fig. 1, bottom.

Remember, the seam will be too close to the back side of the sheath if you mark the hole exactly on the fold. This creates the risk that a gap may form in the seam when the leather dries and stretches. You can eyeball the approximate distance between the holes of the seam if you think this procedure is too difficult. After a little practice on a scrap piece of leather, you will do well. If distances between the holes are not very exact, it shouldn't be a big problem. (Many Sami sew in this manner.)

Certainly it is nice to have perfect sewing, but sometimes it is not possible. Few people will ever see the seam anyway. What is important is that the seam serves its purpose. Do your best and don't be careless! For this type of job, use a straight awl to make holes. In thicker leather, you may need to poke from both sides with the awl to get a sufficiently large hole. Remember that the holes in the wet leather quickly shrink again, so don't make the holes too small.

However, by using a model and making several all-leather sheaths that are exactly the same, you can get a seam that is almost perfect. Prepare a piece of leather in the exact size, so there are no scraps. You can mark the exact spaces for the stitches by using the cardboard model you made to cut appropriately sized pieces of leather. Put that model a few millimeters (¹⁄₁₆ inch) from the leather's edge, exactly parallel to the leather edge on the other side, and use an awl to mark the recess into which the stitch will go.

Fig. 1

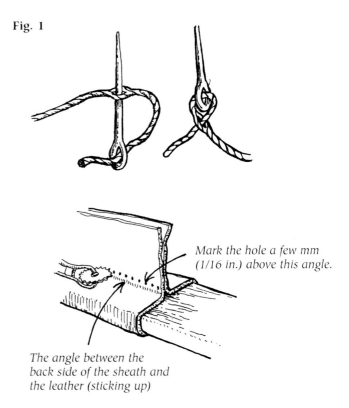

Mark the hole a few mm (1/16 in.) above this angle.

The angle between the back side of the sheath and the leather (sticking up)

You can also make a small marking gauge for the same purpose (Fig. 2). Take two even pieces of wood that are a few centimeters (¾ inch) wide and a few millimeters (¹⁄₁₆ inch) thick. It is sufficient if they are 4 to 5 cm (1½ x 2 inches). Round the front edge of the lower part so it will be easier to follow the curved shapes in the leather. Drill a hole in the upper edge so that a blunt point can be snugly pushed through. The point must reach somewhat below the lower piece. Secure both pieces with a small leather string, and you will have a good marking gauge that makes it easy to make marks in the width you need. To adjust, just loosen the leather string a little, push the pieces towards the end hole, and tie them up again.

After you have scribed a line in the leather, it is easy to use the pricking wheel to mark where you should make the holes with your awl. You could make a fancier stitch, but none will be stronger than this. Do not poke the hole straight through the leather, but rather diagonally, so that the hole will come out in the lower edge of the leather (Fig. 3, left). It can be very tricky to poke all the holes straight the first time. When everything is ready, put the edges against each other and sew them together (Fig. 3, right). If you have done it carefully, the results will match your efforts.

Remember two things: 1. Thin out the edges of the leather before you sew them together (see Fig. 11, page 71). Do not thin to more than half the thickness of the leather. 2. Poke all the holes against a surface that won't damage the point of the awl. The best choice is a plastic or wooden cutting board, or a thick piece of leather or cork.

To ensure that the wood is protected from further damage, cut a shallow notch between the thread holes in the leather. The notches need to be as deep as the thickness of the thread.

Black pitch thread makes your fingers and everything else it touches very black, and it won't come off! Therefore, protect the exposed parts of the sheath with plastic wrap or something similar.

Sew by sticking the needles, one from each side, through the same hole (Fig. 4). The needles should cross each other in the same hole. You will see if the

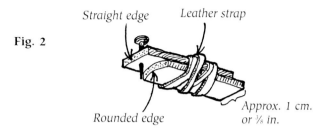

Fig. 2

Straight edge   *Leather strap*

Rounded edge   *Approx. 1 cm. or ⅜ in.*

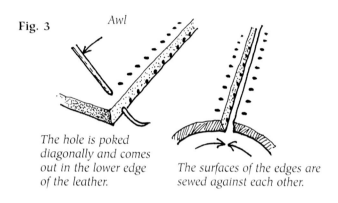

Fig. 3   *Awl*

The hole is poked diagonally and comes out in the lower edge of the leather.   *The surfaces of the edges are sewed against each other.*

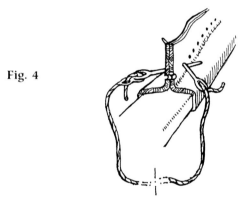

Fig. 4

needles get stuck. (So that the holes aren't too large, I sometimes help the needles out with a pair of flat-nosed pliers.) In order to get a nice stitch, the needles need to go in the holes in the same order the whole time; for example, the left needle always before the right. Sew from the bottom up. In the back edge where you begin sewing, screw a small countersink into the leather so that the thread can sink down into it. In this way, the thread will be protected against further wear and tear. Pull the stitch tight after each hole!

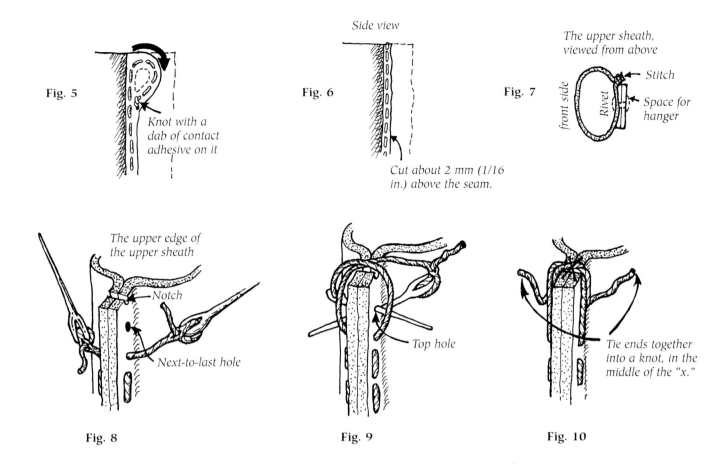

Fig. 5

Knot with a dab of contact adhesive on it

Side view

Fig. 6

Cut about 2 mm (1/16 in.) above the seam.

The upper sheath, viewed from above

Fig. 7

front side *Rivet* Stitch — Space for hanger

The upper edge of the upper sheath

Notch

Next-to-last hole

Fig. 8

Top hole

Fig. 9

Tie ends together into a knot, in the middle of the "x."

Fig. 10

Fig. 11 *Saddler's stitch shown from above (greatly enlarged)*

You can finish off the very top of the leather in various ways, depending on which type of hanger you are using. For the Sami knife, sew up at the very top backwards in a loop that will enclose the opening for the hanger (Fig. 5). Tie a hard knot in the end of the thread and put a dab of contact adhesive on it.

On the other hand, if you are going to rivet the hanger to the back of the upper or lower sheath, end the stitches as in Figs 6 and 7. In this case, the seam would be equally thick all the way. In addition, try to move the stitch to the side so that there will be enough room for the hanger (Fig. 7).

At the top of the leather edge, make a notch or cut to sink the thread into (Fig. 8). Then pull the thread and cross it in the notch before pulling the needles through the top hole (Fig. 9). When you have done this and pulled it out, it should look approximately like Fig 10. Remove the needles when the ends of the thread have gone through the last hole. Tie the ends into a knot at the very top where the thread crosses over in the notch (Fig. 10).

From above, your saddler's stitches should look like the enlargement in Fig. 11.

HAND GUARDS

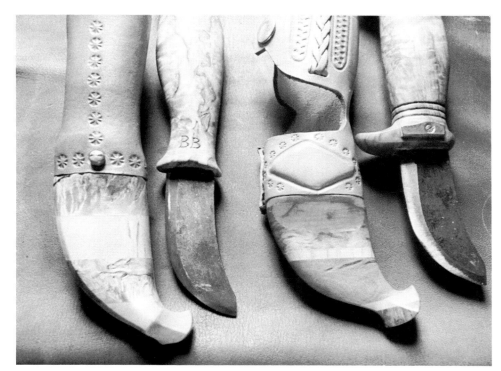

Fig. 2 (above) A short hand guard can sometimes fit inside a sheath.

Fig. 1 The knives on the left will fit into a common sheath, while the one on the right has an extra long finger protector and requires an open type of sheath.

Every year, many people are injured when they use knives without hand guards. A number of these people are even disabled by having their fingers amputated. Accidents happen easily in a moment of forgetfulness, when the hand is wet, or during fishing. These injuries are often hard to treat and sometimes take a long time to heal. Therefore, all knives should have some form of protection. On a woodworking knife that is only used inside the house and is handled by an experienced person, a guard is mainly in the way. But outside the house, the situation may be different.

I suspect that the sometimes negative feelings toward hand guards have to do with the sheath. A knife with a large hand guard can only fit into one kind of sheath—one that only covers the blade (see page 73 for an example). I have compromised on many of my own knives in this respect. It is fine to use most sheath models for knives in which the lower edge of a large hand guard doesn't stick out further

than the broadest point of the handle. See Fig. 2 above. Naturally, it is a compromise, but it's better than nothing. Depending on the shape of the handle, it is sometimes acceptable to make a protector of about 1 cm (⅜ inch) height. The knife will not be completely safe, but better protection requires a double hand guard—then you are locked into one kind of sheath model again.

You should get rid of the habit of sticking the knife into the first piece of wood or stump that comes along. Even if you managed doing this so far, there is no guarantee for the future. Often, the wedged knife tip is stuck so hard that it has to be pried and twisted loose. The tip can then become blunt or damaged, and the blade begins to have a lot of play in the handle. Even as a little boy, I learned to walk with a loose knife with the tip pointed towards the ground and to only place it on a soft surface. This is a lesson you should apply even today.

ALL-LEATHER SHEATHS

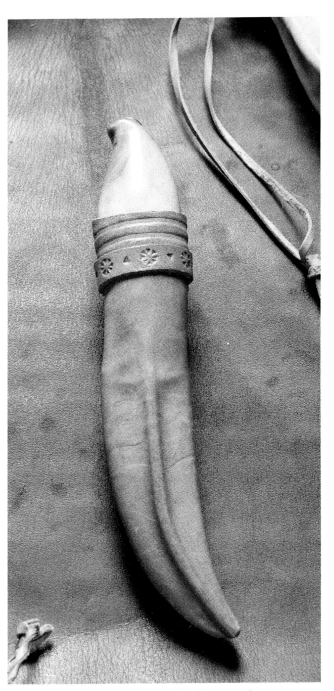

Leather sheath with an inner wooden blade catcher

Leather sheath without a blade catcher

Like handles, knife sheaths can be made from a variety of materials: leather, horn, wood, or a combination of any of these. Perhaps the simplest sheath is the all-leather knife sheath.

You can use an all-leather sheath for any of the knives described thus far. You can use either vegetable-tanned leather or bark-tanned rawhide to make an all-leather sheath, though vegetable-tanned leather is more forgiving. It overlooks small mistakes or errors in calculations, is more stretchy, and, therefore, fits knives that are thicker and more bulky. Sheath leather needs only to be about 2 mm (about 1/16 inch) thick. (Sami knife sheaths are only about half that thick, but are much stronger.) The sheath will become hard as bone and will tolerate a lot. However, fit is very important. The leather doesn't allow mistakes; you must fit to the tenth of a millimeter. Don't let yourself be intimidated! There are ways of meeting the challenge.

For all-leather sheaths, you must first make a wooden model in the shape of your knife to wrap the leather around, which is called a *last*. Or you can make a *blade catcher* of wood and use the handle of the knife as a matching form. We will begin with the blade catcher, which is easier. Before you begin to work, decide which type of leather you want to use.

Vegetable-tanned leather: Wrap the handle with a layer of paper, such as typing paper, before you begin sewing, then wrap the paper with a layer of plastic wrap. This makes the knife easier to remove from the sheath after drying. If you strengthen the inside of the sheath with wood cement and press it hard against greaseproof paper, the sheath will have a smooth interior.

Bark-tanned rawhide: Wrap the handle with two to three layers of paper, then with a layer of plastic wrap. When you take the knife out after a couple of days, the sheath will be too large. Let the sheath dry a few more days without the knife in it, and it will shrink to almost the exact fit. When you use this leather, the upper edge of the sheath must end just a couple of millimeters (about 1/16 inch) above the thickest part of the handle. Then the knife will fit perfectly in the sheath. Soften the leather for at least an hour.

LEATHER SHEATH WITH INNER BLADE CATCHER

Take two pieces of wood and saw each to 2 to 3 cm (3/4 to 1 1/4 inches) larger than the dimensions of the blade. Sand the surfaces that will be placed against each other so that they are flat, using coarse sandpaper on the bench (Fig. 1). Place the knife blade on one of the two surfaces. Draw a line about 2 to 3 mm (about 1/16 to 1/8 inch) outside the outer contours of the blade (Fig. 2). Rotate the blade and draw a line on the other sanded piece. Using a sharp knife, cut along the contours as deeply as you can (Fig. 3).

Fig. 1 *Use coarse sandpaper to flatten the facing surfaces.*

Fig. 2 *Mark the area to be hollowed out for the blade.*

Fig. 3 *Cut along the contours.*

Use a chisel to cut out the wood between the contours (Fig. 4). Use the knife again to go deeper—about 3 to 4 mm (about 5/32 inch) into both pieces of wood. Make sure that the bottom of each piece is as level and uniformly deep as possible. Turn one of the pieces and mark the outer contours of your sheath. Saw off the excess wood. Then glue the two pieces together (using wood cement) and apply pressure.

When the cement has hardened, saw off the excess from the other piece as well. Use the first piece as a guide (Fig. 5). Round the outside with a knife, file, and rasp (Figs. 6 and 7). Grease the wood with boiled linseed oil or paraffin oil. Insert the knife into the blade catcher and measure (on a sheet of paper) how much leather is needed (Fig. 8). Wrap the piece of leather around the blade catcher to test it. You will probably want to use vegetable-tanned

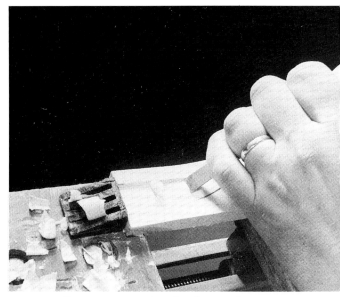
Fig. 4 *Hollow out area with a chisel or similar tool.*

Fig. 5

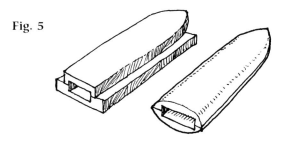

Fig. 6

Fig. 7 *Make the back side level, and form a ridge on the front.*

leather. Soften the leather five to ten minutes in luke-warm water. Center it over your wooden blade catcher and begin to sew it together, using a saddler's stitch (see page 54 and Fig. 9). When you have sewn up to the handle of the knife, insert the knife into the blade catcher. It should remain there until the leather has dried (Fig. 10). (Oil or grease the blade first, so that it doesn't rust from moisture.)

Continue to sew upwards. When you have reached .5 cm (1/4 inch) from the upper edge, sew outward, then backward and downward, forming a half-heart shape (Fig. 11). Tie a knot (see Fig. 13).

The sheath leather should now have the exact shape as your knife. It is usually easiest to decorate the sheath a few hours after you have sewn the leather (Fig. 12). (See page 76.)

60

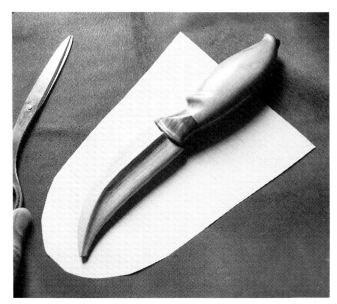

Fig. 8 *Estimate how much leather you will need with paper, then cut out the leather.*

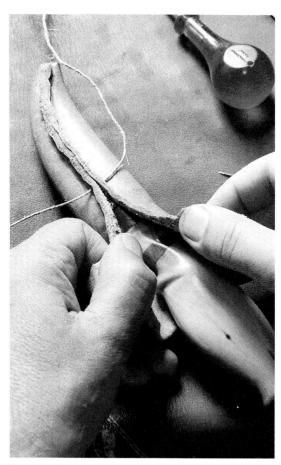

Fig. 10 *Insert the knife when the stitches reach the edge of the blade catcher.*

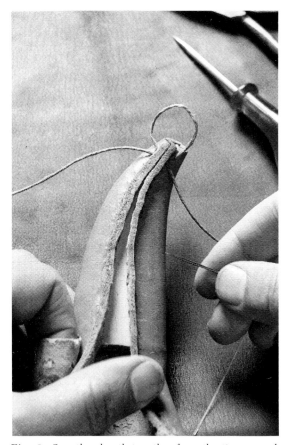

Fig. 9 *Sew the sheath together from the tip upwards.*

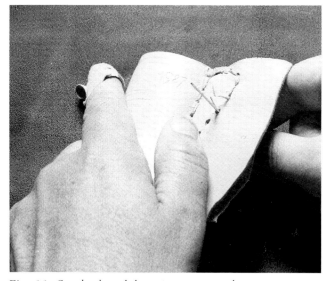

Fig. 11 *Sew back and down in a curve at the very top.*

61

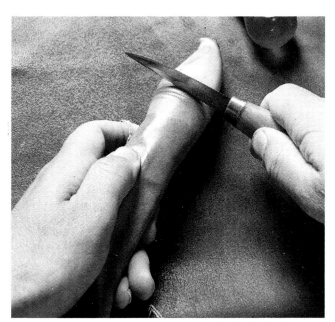

Fig. 12 *Decorating the sheath with the back of a knife*

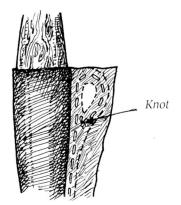

Knot

Fig. 13

Fig. 14 *Prepare the leather hanger and tie off.*

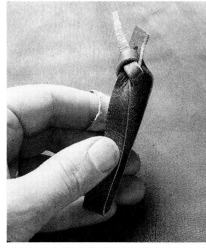

Fig. 15 *Thin, twined-leather hanger*

When the leather has dried a couple of days at room temperature, cut a hole inside the seam for the hanger (Fig. 13) and cut off the excess leather a few millimeters (about 1/16 inch) outside the stitches. Make sure that there is a hole far down in the leather tip, and that it goes through both the leather and the wood. You can make the hanger by various methods. Here are two suggestions.

SUGGESTIONS FOR HANGERS

Cut a leather strap (about 25 cm or 10 inches long and 10 cm or 4 inches wide) out of the sheath leather. Make an approximately 2-cm-long (3/4-inch) cut into the middle of the strap, longitudinal to the strap, about 1.5 cm (1/2 inch) from one end. Thread the strap into a hole behind the knife, and tie it as shown in Fig. 14.

For the other method, use a thinner leather strap (1 mm or ¹⁄₃₂ inch) that is approximately 1 m (3¼ feet) long. Soften it well and twine it together along its entire length. Twist to the right. Squeeze the strap in the middle, without letting go of the end of the strap, causing it to roll together. Thread it through the hole on the back end of the sheath and tie it together (Fig. 15). See page 74 for other hanger suggestions.

LEATHER SHEATH WITHOUT BLADE CATCHER

First, make a full-scale wooden model of your knife and sketch a model on paper. Allow a good amount of space around the knife, or the edge will cut the inside of the leather every time you take the knife out or put it back. Carve a model out of easy-to-carve wood that is as long as the sheath. Add a few centimeters (¾ inch) above the upper edge of the sheath to grip when removing the model after the leather has dried (Fig. 16).

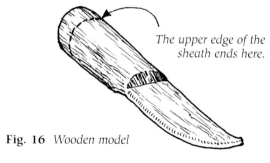

The upper edge of the sheath ends here.

Fig. 16 *Wooden model*

This type of sheath can give beginners a headache. The handle of the wooden model must be exactly the same shape and thickness as your knife (Figs. 17 and 18). A good eyeball measurement is a big help, and a sliding caliper can tell whether the handle model's depth and side measurements agree. But you won't get the circumference with a caliper. Use thick sewing thread and take measurements on various parts of the knife handle. Then transfer these to the wooden model. Hold the thread firmly so it doesn't slide!

Slowly work your way up to the correct circumference by rasping or filing off a little, then measuring. Eventually, you should have a model that generally

matches your knife—at least in respect to the handle. If your model is a little too thick at the top, the knife will sink too far down into the sheath. If it is too narrow, the knife will sit too high. The latter is preferable, because you can soften the leather again and stretch out the sheath.

Fig. 17 *Knife and the finished model*

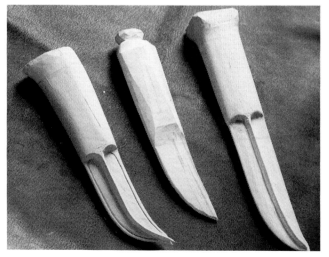

Fig. 18 *Examples of other wooden models*

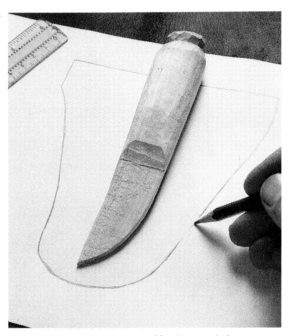

Fig. 19 *Sketch the amount of leather needed on paper.*

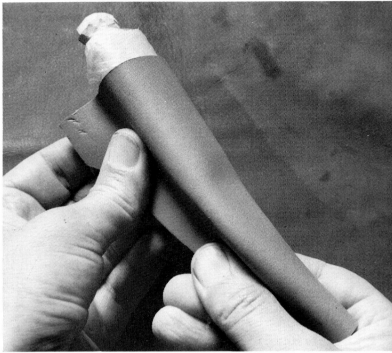

Fig. 21 *Shape the leather and stretch it around the model.*

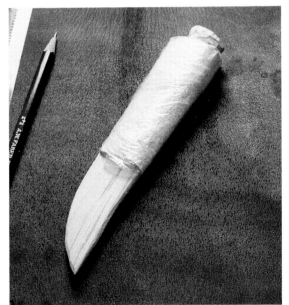

Fig. 20 *Wrap the model with plastic wrap and paper.*

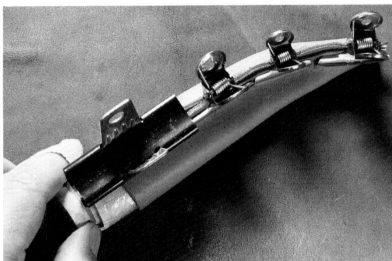

Fig. 22 *Glue clamps in place*

Using the wooden model, shape the knife sheath. The sheath will look clumsy if the blade of the model is too thick—5 mm or ¹¹/₆₄ inch is sufficient. A smoother surface on the model makes it easier to get the sheath loose after drying. It is a also good idea to grease the model with boiled linseed oil or paraffin oil. The knife will be easy to take out of the sheath if the model can be divided in the middle and

is a few millimeters larger (¹/₁₆ inch) than the knife. Using a pencil, trace the size of the leather you will need on a piece of paper, then cut it out (Fig. 19). While the leather is softening, thread two saddler's needles with pitch thread, waxed linen thread, or sinew thread. Genuine sinew thread is the best and strongest thread, followed by pitch thread. (Black pitch blackens the leather and the marks are almost

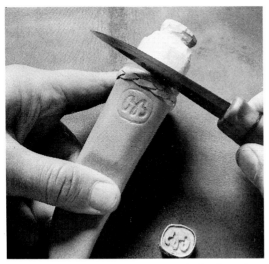

Fig. 23 *Decorate with the back of a knife and a wooden stamp.*

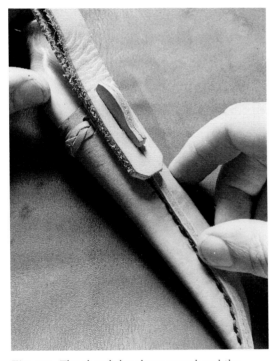

Fig. 25 *The sheath has been sewed and the hanger mounted.*

impossible to remove. Soften vegetable leather five to ten minutes in lukewarm water and Sami leather at least an hour. With Sami leather, the handle of the model must be wrapped with two to three layers of paper and a layer of plastic wrap (Fig. 20).

Shape the wet, soft leather around the model (Fig. 21). It helps to clamp the end of the model into a vise, so that the model is horizontal. Then look to see to which direction the leather bends easiest—up and down or crosswise—before you wrap it around the model. Make sure that it relaxes and conforms to all the contours of the model. Use all the strength in your fingers to stretch the leather out on the back side of the sheath where the seam will be. After a while, when the leather has completely taken the shape of the model, begin to attach the leather with glue clamps on the back side (Fig. 22). Make sure that the leather is stretched the whole time. (At least ten glue clamps are needed.) The clamps should sit edge-to-edge along the entire back side. The ones that go on the inward and outward curves are the most important clamps. Glue clamps must get as close to the model as possible all the way down. After a few hours, you can decorate the leather without disturbing the glue clamps (Fig. 23). Then leave it to dry for a couple of days.

If the tip of the model's blade is completely straight, sew directly with saddler's stitches as close to the model as possible; you will not need glue clamps. But if the tip

Fig. 24

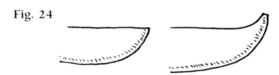

is a little curved at the bottom (Fig. 24) and you sew in this way, you will never get the knife out when the leather is dry. After drying, sew together the side with saddler's stitches exactly like the previous leather sheath (see page 56). Mount the hanger (Fig. 25).

When you have more experience sewing, you can try sewing without a needle. Apply wax or quick-drying glue on the tips of the thread. When it hardens, sew as usual. One advantage to using this method is that you will need fewer holes in the side seam. The model must remain in the sheath while you sew. Cut a small hole in the tip of the leather for air, and for use as a drain hole.

If the stitches are too loose, there will be space between the leather surfaces when the sheath dries. If the sheath is sewed around the model from the start, it is sometimes a little difficult to remove the model from the sheath after drying. If so, tap it with a hammer on the upper part of the handle where the hanger will be and against the upper edge of the front side, placing a small piece of wood in between as protection.

MIXED-MATERIAL SHEATHS

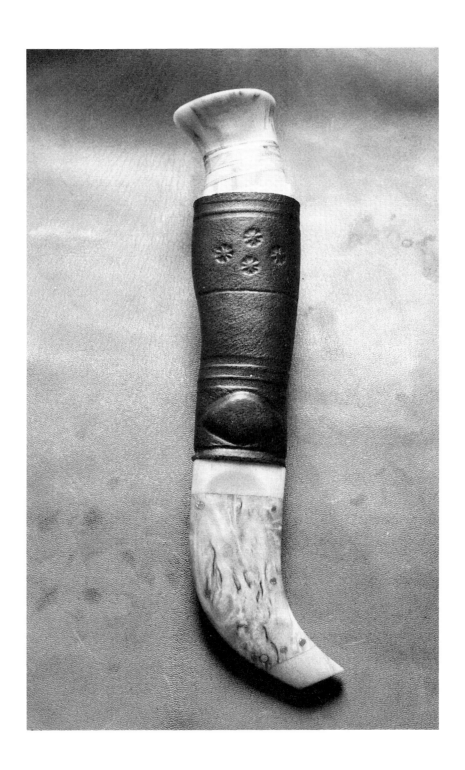

In this knife sheath, the lower part is made of curly grained birch and riveted with copper wire.

This section describes how to make a horn sheath that has an upper part made of leather, one of the most common types of Sami knife sheaths.

You will need a broad, thin piece of the reindeer's antler, preferably one found directly beyond the rosenkrans, or the part of the antler that is closest to the head of the reindeer (see page 12). The best pieces are found, as I mentioned before, on the antlers of large reindeer bucks that have been slaughtered. The knife sheath is a little harder to make than the Sami handle. Don't let this intimidate you, but do expect some challenges.

Either saw your own antler piece or mail-order the correct size. (When ordering, specify what the piece will be used for.) The length of the blade determines the length of the antler piece. Depending on what kind of a piece you get, you can make the more curved model of the north-Sami type, or the more bow-shaped, southern type.

A wooden sheath with a leather upper part is unfortunately not very common today. As far as I know, there are not many factory-made knives that use this combination. Knifemakers in the countryside are probably the main producers of them. Sometimes, you will see Sami knives with sheaths made of wood. Most often, it is for a large, long, and powerful knife that the Sami use for everything from branding calves to axes. A wooden sheath is probably not as strong as one of antler, but the wood is much kinder to the edges of the knives and weighs considerably less.

The wooden sheath has become something of a favorite of mine. Because such a sheath is often made of the same wood as the knife, the knife and sheath form a harmonious unit. Sometimes, I make the entire wooden part of the sheath in curly grained birch, then put common birch on the back. One advantage of wooden sheaths is that there is not much scrap. Sometimes, the pieces that were sawed off the knife handle—that would have been thrown away—are enough to make a sheath.

LOWER HORN PART

Clamp the horn in a vise, with pieces of leather on each side for protection, and cut it with a hacksaw (or band saw) into two halves; if the halves are too thick, thin them with a rasp. Rasp the edges to achieve the correct appearance. Then make adjustments so that the insides fit flush against each other. For the most part, you should know how you want your sheath to look now: how sharp the curve should be, how wide the sheath should be at the bottom, and so on.

Put your knife blade against one half of the inside and sketch the contours. Do the same with the other half. Shape the contours of the sheath, using a knife, chisel, or a power drill with a cone-shaped mill attachment. If you use a drill, hold it towards the sheath and the edge, and cut along the track (Fig. 1). Hold both the drill and the piece you are working on. A flexible axle on the drill is nice, but a chisel or knife also works well. It is a matter of removing the marrow. The outside must be secured, or the edges will split. Sand the insides completely flat with sandpaper, brush them off, then glue the sides together with epoxy glue (Fig. 4, page 69). When this has hardened, drill the drain hole vertically down from the bottom of the sheath (see Fig. 1).

For the halves to stay together, they must be riveted with copper or brass wire (1.5-mm [⁵⁄₆₄-inch] or 16-gauge wire is sufficient). Drill holes of exactly the same measurements to rivet through on both halves (Fig. 5, page 69). Riveting is only necessary on the lower part; the upper part is held together by the leather portion of the sheath.

Fig. 1

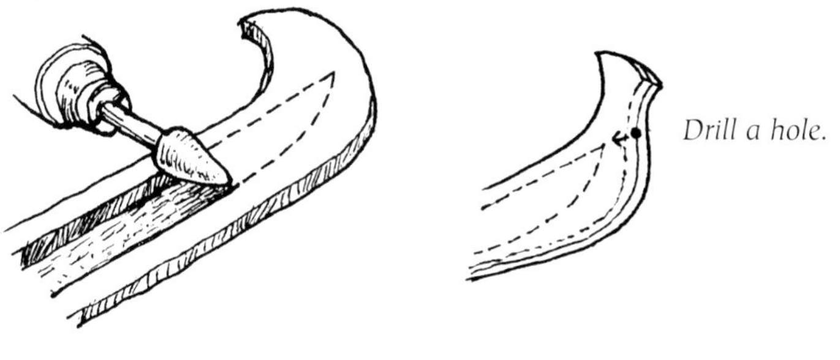

Drill a hole.

67

Make sure that the rivets do not go inside the sheath, but only through solid horn along the edges. Put a piece of wire into the hole and cut it so that a maximum of 1 mm (⅟₃₂ inch) sticks out (Fig. 6, page 69). Rivet the front side first. (No matter what you do, the first rivet always seems to work best.) Tap carefully with a ball peen hammer in the middle of the surface of the wire and make sure that the back side of the wire lies against the vise (Fig. 7, page 69). It is OK to improvise in an emergency. I have riveted against a pipe stump, the edge of the kitchen sink, an iron lever, and so on. Make sure not to hit the outside of the horn, because any marks will not go away. The horn part of the sheath is now almost finished.

Fasten the leather portion of the sheath to the horn in one of several ways. Insert the knife in the sheath and use a pencil to trace around the end of the handle, toward the upper part of the lower sheath. Then bevel the upper part to that measured area. Begin gradually a couple of centimeters (¾ inch) down where the beveling ends with a soft, rounded edge made with a round file. Save some horn so you can make a round or square "button" to attach to the leather (see Fig. 2, left), in which you have made a hole of the same diameter. Drill a loose rivet and glue it into place later, if that is easier. For even better fastening and aesthetic value, shape a fold at the bottom of the notch, but only on the front and sides. Another method is to leave a "ridge" at the top of the sheath, for the leather to adhere to. Make the ridge a maximum of 5 mm (¹¹⁄₆₄ inches) thick. Then you can leave out the "button" if you want (Figs. 8 and 9, page 69).

The most beautiful sheath will be the one with several indentations, perhaps in two to three places to replace both the button and the ridge. These are made as deep as the thickness of the leather and are only made on the front side and the side edges. Look at pictures of Sami knives for several more elegant solutions.

Finally, the horn portion of the sheath needs to be polished. Put your heart and soul into doing a fine job. The horn should shine and have luster, and be completely free of scratches.

LOWER WOOD PART

You make the wooden sheath using the same method as the horn sheath, but you will have two wooden halves instead (Fig. 3, below). Make the indentation for the knife with a chisel, then cut out the contours of the blade with a sharp knife. You can also make attachments (buttons or ridges) for a leather handle. The wooden sheath is finished in the same way as the wooden handle.

UPPER LEATHER PART

To make the upper leather part, use Sami knife leather, or specially tanned cowhide. Measure how high you want the leather to go, using a piece of paper (Fig. 10). On a Sami knife, it usually goes 3 to 4 cm (1¼ to 1½ inches) from the back end of the

Fig. 3 *Carve out a space for the blade in both halves.*

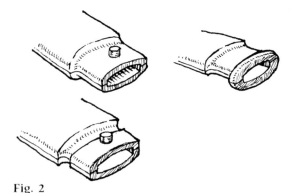

Fig. 2

68

Fig. 4 *Glue the halves together, applying pressure.*

Fig. 5 *Gently make a hole for the rivets.*

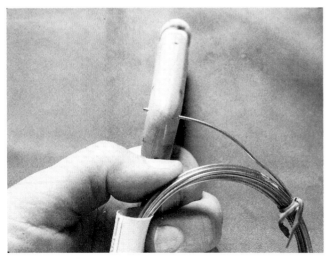

Fig. 6 *Put copper wire through the hole.*

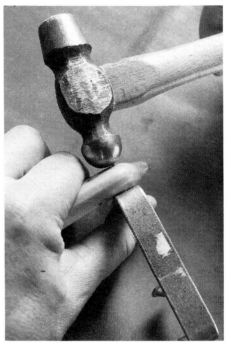

Fig. 7 *Rivet the wire against a hard surface.*

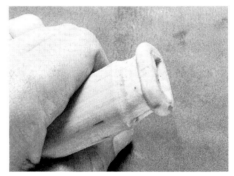

Fig. 8 *Make a groove in the upper part of the wood or horn section.*

Fig. 9 *A differently shaped "button"*

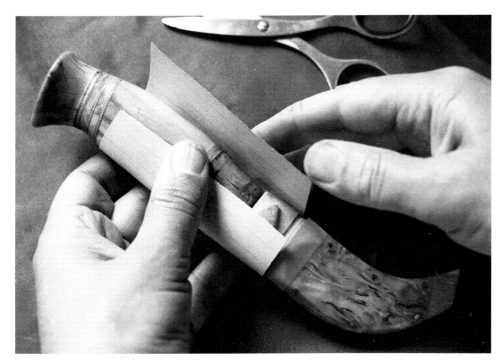

Fig. 10 *Use a piece of paper to determine how much leather you will need.*

handle, provided the handle is not too oval. Make sure that it reaches all the way around and that there are at least 3 cm (1¼ inches) extra on each side when you pinch it together. Soften the piece of leather for approximately an hour, bending it occasionally so that it will be supple. Thin the edges, using a regular knife or a flaking knife, so that it will not be as thick to sew through on the back side (see Fig. 11).

Put the knife in the sheath. Wrap no more than two or three layers of thin paper around the handle; then do the same with a thin layer of plastic wrap. This is so that the leather part of the sheath will not be too tight. Put the straight, even edges against the beveled-off edge of leather (Fig. 12). (Watch for where you are going to make a hole for the button.) Pinch together and stretch the leather on the back side. Sew from the bottom up, using sinew thread or pitch thread (Fig. 13). Sew short, tight stitches and stretch the leather the entire time, as you move upwards (Fig. 14). Keep the needle as close to the handle as possible, and pull the thread all the way out. At the top, the seam should go back into a loop (Fig. 15). Tie the ends of the thread. Cut off the leather outside the seam with a sharp knife, 2 to 3 mm (⁵⁄₆₄ to ⅛ inch) from the stitches. Then make the hole for the hanger.

Pinch around the beveled-off edge. Take the back side of a knife and push and pull it across the beveling. You can also pull a string tight on each beveled-off edge, and remove it when the leather has dried. If you would like, decorate the front side of the upper sheath—with the back of a knife, for example. If you want to do more decoration, do it now (see the section on decorations on page 76).

Let the leather dry at room temperature; do not use a radiator. A couple of days usually suffices. Then hold the sheath against your cheek. There is still moisture in it if it feels cold. Otherwise, take out the knife and remove the paper and plastic. Let the sheath dry a few more days, then test the fit again. Due to variations in the leather, it is hard to say how many layers of paper are needed. You must test your way along. If the fit wasn't good the first time, you can soften the leather sheath again, and either stretch it out a little or squeeze it together. Make the hanger to carry the knife, using one of the methods described in the section on page 74. Provided everything has gone well, now you can put your signature on the back side of the sheath and proudly carry your knife.

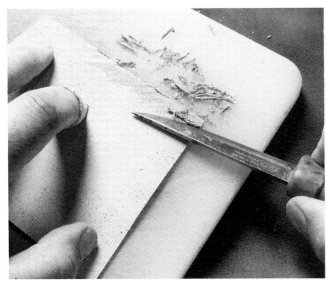

Fig. 11 *Thin out the thick leather along the edges with a sharp knife.*

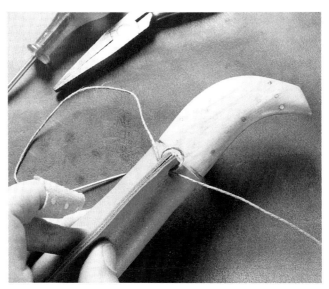

Fig. 13 *Begin sewing at the bottom.*

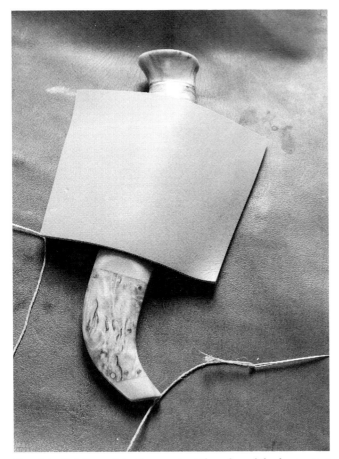

Fig. 12 *Put the soft leather against the edge of the lower part.*

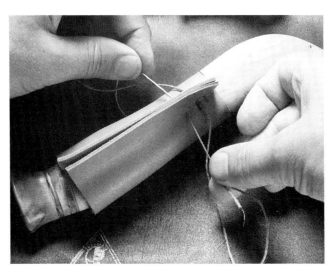

Fig. 14 *Sew upward. The two needles are pushed in through the same hole from opposite directions.*

Fig. 15 *Sew a loop.*

ALL-WOOD SHEATHS

If you succeed in getting a long enough piece of beautiful wood (about 20 cm or 8 inches), you can make an all-wood sheath. Preferably, the knife and the sheath should be of the same type of wood. It is also important for the handle portion to be sufficiently thick. In this model, the entire handle can fit into the sheath. This sheath is made of two halves, exactly like the earlier sheaths. When you trace the sheath from the side, remember to leave plenty of wood around the handle to allow for a margin for error. The hollowed-out area for the blade and handle are made as already described, using knives, chisels, and possibly a round carving iron (see page 60). A narrow opening on each side of the part that covers the handle is necessary for making space for the handle (Fig. 1, left). This space allows the upper part to bend to the inside and outside when the handle is inserted into the sheath. Do a good job on this part. Test it often and make small incisions every time. The tang has to squeeze in once the thickest part of the handle is in. Do not forget to make a drain hole at the bottom—at least 3 mm (⅛ inch) in diameter.

You will need to rivet at regular intervals along the entire length of the sheath. Just as with wood and leather sheaths, you can rivet this sheath with wooden pins instead of metal. If you are using wooden pins, first decide what diameter of pins you need, for example 3 mm (⅛ inch). Drill holes in the right places along the edges of the sheath, using a 3-mm (⅛-inch) drill bit. Carve the pins out of very hard wood—birch, for example. Make them slightly conical. They can be 3 to 4 mm (⅛ to 5/32 inch) thick. Then take a 1-cm-thick (⅜-inch) piece of very hard wood. Drill a hole through the piece of wood, using a 3-mm (⅛-inch) drill bit. Insert one conical pin at a time into these holes, driving them through. Use a round piercer of some kind, and pound with the hammer. Put the pins directly into the sheath. They will swell up to regain their thickness of about 4 mm (5/32 inch).

Make the outside of the sheath any way you would like. You have a very large surface to work on, so you don't have to make it all flat. Let your creativity and imagination go to work!

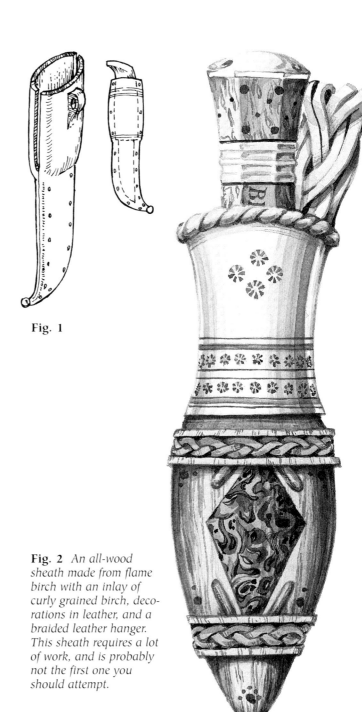

Fig. 1

Fig. 2 *An all-wood sheath made from flame birch with an inlay of curly grained birch, decorations in leather, and a braided leather hanger. This sheath requires a lot of work, and is probably not the first one you should attempt.*

72

SIMPLE SHEATHS

If you think the knife sheaths I have discussed so far are difficult, here are a few simple sheaths.

SHEATHS FOR KNIVES WITH HAND GUARDS

Knives with hand guards (see page 57) require specially shaped sheaths. First, sketch and cut out a paper pattern that fits your knife. Using the pattern, cut the sheath out of leather. Fold the lower part, mark

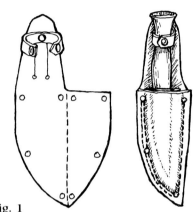

Fig. 1

holes for rivets (Fig. 1), then make the holes with a hollow punch or punching tongs. Cut slits that are the width of your belt in the upper section. A 2-mm ($\frac{1}{16}$-inch) hole (punched with a hollow punch) in the ends prevents the notches from being worn out over time (See Fig. 1). Cut a leather strip that is long enough to wrap around the knife handle. Rivet the middle of the lower part, and test with your knife to determine where the snap should go. Sew along the edges of the sheath with double saddler's stitches. Then rivet the sheath together in the ready-made holes.

These are only general principles; you can vary the pattern, according to your own taste. Remember to always practice first with a paper pattern.

SHEATHS FOR KNIVES WITHOUT HAND GUARDS

Use a paper pattern that fits the knife you are using exactly. The pattern can be varied, according to your own taste. To make one of the sheaths in Fig. 2, cut it out, then sew, rivet, design, and soften. To get a sheath with a perfect fit, insert the oiled knife into the sheath and let it stay there until the leather is dry. If you think it is hard to make the sewing look nice at first, thread the edges together with a *splicing strap*, or a continuous 3-mm-wide ($\frac{1}{8}$-inch) leather strap

used to wrap the edge. Make holes with a hollow punch or a thonging chisel for the bridge seam (see tools for working with leather, page 17). Fig. 3 (right) demonstrates this method of sewing sheaths.

To construct an excellent type of sheath that is relatively easy to make (provided your knife does not have too long of a hand guard or finger protector), sew with a double-stitch and rivet the edge in three places (Fig. 2). The opening should be a little narrower than it is with the other rivets. The finger protector should fit just below the top, where it should rest approximately flush with the other rivets with exactly enough space for the knife to move. You will have to test as you go, using your own knife to find the best places for the rivets.

The leather stretches a little with time, so it doesn't matter if it is tight at first. Do not forget to insert a plastic knife-edge guard, or to make your own from wood.

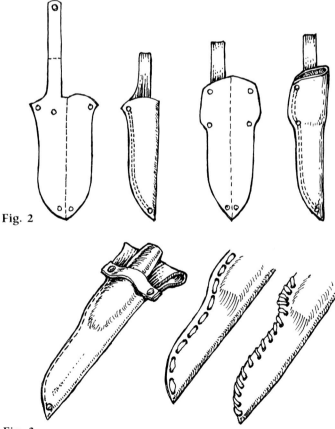

Fig. 2

Fig. 3

HANGERS

Fig. 1 shows various types of hanging devices. I do not offer general advice about which type of hanger is best, since this often depends on individual habits and desires. Some people are happy with a very mobile knife; others want more control over it.

Hangers A and B allow knives easy movement. The advantage to using these is that the knife never gets in the way, no matter how much you move. The disadvantage is that the knife can be a little hard to get to. It is also somewhat difficult to pull the knife out with one hand if the knife sits tightly in the sheath.

If you are in doubt, consider this: A Sami knife nearly always has hanger A. Few use the knife as a work tool more than the Sami. For hundreds of years, their knives have hung on twined belts of reindeer skin. If there had been a better solution, this method would have been replaced. The Sami have probably tested most other solutions and rejected them. A hanger twined with double hide straps, with a knot that is glued, should not fall apart. Lost knives probably result more from misplacing knives than from the hanger coming loose.

I frequently use hanger A, and I like it well. The knife comes out with lightning speed, except when you are sitting on the ground or in a car. In these cases, you still can get it out easily, though the sheath must be moved around on the belt.

I am convinced that a knife that can be removed with one hand has to sit dangerously loose in the sheath. In my opinion, it should not be possible to pull any knife out with one hand and, if it is, there is a problem with the fit of the knife in the sheath. None of the types shown in Fig. 1 allow the knife to be drawn with one hand. The only way to do this would be to have a holder in the lower part of the sheath that properly tightens with a belt around the thigh. Only then is it possible.

Hangers B and C are among the most common designs. Hanger C is the most stable of the first three; hanger D has a closed hook and a snap hook so that the knife can be quickly unhooked from the belt; hanger E is approximately as stable and strong as hanger C. By moving the seam on the back as far down as it can go, you get a broad surface for a really strong hanger. Hanger F is completely without metal

Fig. 1

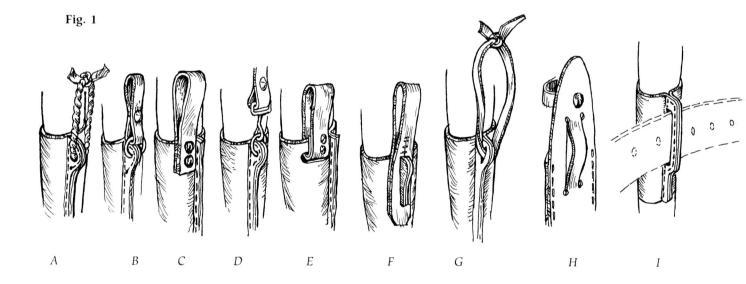

| A | B | C | D | E | F | G | H | I |

parts. Once the hanger fits the hanging hook exactly—without play or space in between—it is sewed and becomes safe and secure (Fig. 2). I often make this type of hanger from strong vegetable leather. Hanger G is a simple, but effective and strong hanger, if it is tied right (see page 62 for how to tie this hanger). Hanger H is the model found on belt covers for folding knives, and on *scout knifes*. The sheath comes up higher than the other models, moves a little, and is perhaps a little more out of the way. In my opinion, the disadvantage is that the knife falls uncomfortably high, and when you go to take it out of the sheath, it has a tendency to bend in the middle. The belt case for folding knives works the same way. Because of stiff leather and immobility, they usually poke you in the small of your back when you sit down. Finally, hanger I consists of a slit in a size that fits your belt. With this hanger, the knife does not move very much.

Test the various hanger types as you go to discover your favorite hanger type. A cautious first recommendation regarding hangers A or G: if you are really handy, you can mount a clamp on the hanger and make the length adjustable.

Fig. 2 *Detail of hanger F*

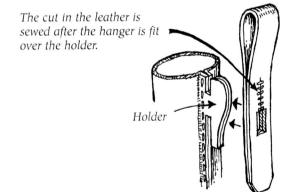

The cut in the leather is sewed after the hanger is fit over the holder.

Holder

RIVETS AND SNAPS

You may need a rivet to attach a hanger to the sheath. For this, a two-part rivet is used, or a *double hollow rivet*. They come in several sizes. Ones 10.5 x 10 mm (or about $^{13}/_{32}$ x $^{3}/_{8}$ inch) are common for such purposes. Double hollow rivets can be purchased with nickel plating, covered with brass, or oxidated. The latter two provide the best protection against rust. At the same time, they don't dominate the appearance of your work as much, and their color is beautiful against the leather. The rivet parts are pounded together against a metal surface. A tripod stand works best, but either an anvil or an iron lever will work. Pound with a metal hammer in the middle of the rivet head. Fit them well, so that the parts don't end up askew. A hand tool used for rivets of various sizes works best. Such tools will not deform the head of the rivet and are inexpensive.

Snaps for knife sheaths should be strong. In hard leather, a snap that will not come open at the slightest movement is necessary if you don't want to lose the knife. A snap is made in four parts that are installed in a specific order. Special tools are needed for this. All of these things are available in ready-made packages sold in department and hardware stores. The tool is good enough to be used on several snaps, so once you have purchased the first package, you need only to replenish the parts. A hard surface is needed for this, too. Follow the manufacturer's instructions.

DECORATIONS

Fig. 1 *An assortment of home-made tools have been used to decorate leather; everything from the heads of nails to buttons, coins, and medals can also be used, though any text comes out as mirror images. Wooden stamps are easy to make, for example, with initials. Circles can be made with a dull hollow punch. Let your imagination find new tools!*

Many knifemakers like to put some form of decoration on the leather part of sheaths (Fig. 1). The greatest risk is overdecorating—not the opposite. Leather surfaces that are completely undecorated can have their own distinct beauty. Especially if the horn or wooden part of the sheath is decorated, a heavily decorated upper sheath takes away from the overall impression. Be moderate and you will get the best results.

Both vegetable-tanned leather and bark-tanned rawhide can be decorated, though it is easiest to shape and decorate vegetable-tanned leather. It is important that the leather you wish to decorate is not dyed with leather dye or treated with a finishing of any sort.

With vegetable leather, the impression penetrates more deeply and remains more distinct after drying. Put patterns on vegetable leather when you are finished sewing the sheath. While the leather is still wet, mark the decorations carefully with your

tools (Fig. 2). Not much of the first marking will remain while the leather is soaked through. After approximately four hours of air drying, go over the entire impression again and determine where the decoration or lines will go. Now you have an impression that will be deep and lasting. A few hours later, go over all of it one more time. After the final drying, most of the design will remain. You can wait a few hours with Sami knife leather, or simply soften the surface for another day, then decorate.

There are numerous methods for making decorative patterns. If you want to go deeper into the subject, refer to a book on leather handiwork. Nearly all objects will make some impression on leather surfaces. Wet leather is like a wet, smooth clay surface. Working against a hard surface makes the impression go deeper. Many household objects can be used: nails, screws, empty ballpoint pens, knitting needles, forks, metal netting, screwdrivers, and so on. Take the

Fig. 2 *Making a groove with a homemade wooden border-edge marker*

piece of wood, then press it into your leather. Don't forget to cut the letters and characters in mirror images with the letters raised over the surface.

One decorating method I advise against is "burn marking" or drawing on the leather with heat. This is done with a soldering iron or heat-drawing device. In both cases, you destroy the surface of the leather and the work easily assumes a mass-production look.

INLAYS

Perhaps you have seen beautiful knives with inlays, and want to attempt to do something similar with your own knife. I do not have any great experience with inlays, but here is a simple method you can use.

You can inlay with both wood and horn. It is easiest to do inlaying on a level surface; it takes significantly longer on a curved surface. First, sketch a pattern on cardboard or paper in the shape you want the inlay. Then put the pattern in exactly the place where the inlay will be and trace along the edges. Make the inlay piece first! Sand its edges so that they are completely even. For straight edges, lay it against something, such as a table knife, and test it. Allow for inlay gluing margins in the measurement so you can adjust, about 2 mm ($\frac{1}{16}$ inch) thick. Put the finished piece into place and mark the contours accurately on the surface underneath. Then cut along the pencil lines and remove the wood in between with a chisel, down to about 1.5 mm ($\frac{3}{64}$ inch) deep. Check to see if the piece fits perfectly and tightly in all corners. Pointy and conical areas are the hardest to fit. Adjust very carefully. Beveling the inlay piece a little along its edges will increase your chances of succeeding.

Then fit and glue the piece tightly into place with pressure. Be careful not to split it. For reinforcement, you can rivet your piece with metal or wood. Brass screws also work well. When it has dried, the inlay will sit a little higher, because it is a little thicker. Sand it down to make it flush with its surroundings.

If you feel a little unsure, but still want to try it, first attempt inlaying on a scrap piece. The experience you gain will be invaluable.

time to test a scrap piece of leather just to get a feel for the work.

You can also make many pattern-making tools. File a pattern on the head of a nail and make impressions with it. Position the tool and pound with a hammer. Patterns can be made with the ends of round wooden dowels. File the end of a crochet hook or a plastic handle. Saw off a piece of horn and carve something on the level surface. Feel free to experiment; there are no fixed rules. Avoid buying expensive factory-made punches for making impressions in leather; they are made of metal and plastic and only provide a standard selection of impressions, such as stars, flowers, and so forth.

When using larger tools to make patterns—for example, coins, medals, and company logo markers—you must press the tool into the leather with a vise. Put the tool against one jaw, the leather in the middle, and a hard rubber or wooden board against the other jaw. Tighten it well! Let it sit a while before you loosen it. The leather must be damp. Remember, any text will appear as mirror images on the leather.

If you are handy with a knife, you can carve out your initials or a date on the end surface of a hard

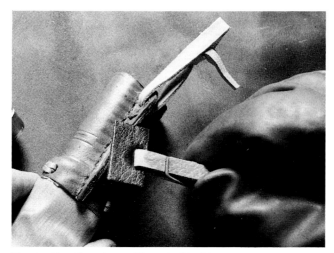

Fig. 3 *Dye the edges with grain blacking.*

Fig. 4 *Apply beeswax.*

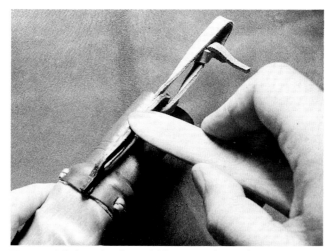

Fig. 5 *Polish with a bone folder or similar tool.*

DYEING

Dyeing leather could be an entire chapter on its own, so I suggest you refer to any of the excellent books on the subject for more detailed information.

Nevertheless, I can't help but mention the importance of dyeing all the edges on your leather work. Many knifemakers dye the edges but hardly any of them use wax to treat them. All the edges can be dyed, preferably black. Do this with black leather dye, which is called *grain blacking* (Fig. 3). The cheapest tool you can use for this is a piece of felt that is held by a clothespin.

In order to achieve hard, shiny, and smooth surfaces, rub the edges of the corner with polishing wax or beeswax (Fig. 4). Use leather grease next, then polish the edges until they are hard and shiny. For polishing, you should use a bone folder (Fig. 5). You can also use a flat piece of wood with a soft, rounded edge, the back of a comb, the handle of a toothbrush, or something similar. There are many good substitutions for a bone folder, as long as they are hard, smooth, and don't tear the leather. This job takes a little time, but don't give up before the fiber residue is gone.

CARE

MAINTAINING HANDLES AND SHEATHS

Your knife will not require much care when it is finished, whether it is made of wood or leather. But here are a few things to think about. Treating previously oiled wood occasionally helps reduce the risk of splits forming, among other things. After the original oil hardens (in a week), continue to rub oil into the wood surfaces almost every day for the next few days, then approximately once a month for the first year. Dry off any excess oil.

The leather in the sheath contains tanning material that has a tendency to rub off on the fittings—including the brass ferrules, which will become coated with verdigris. This residue also causes carbonized steel blades to rust. This is how knives become coated with verdigris and rust inside the house. Thus, never allow the knife to sit in the sheath when you are at home. Rain makes the sheath moist, so let it sit at room temperature until it is almost dry. Then apply leather waterproofing of the type you grease leather shoes with. Next time, it will accommodate the water much better. Don't forget to wash and dry the knife after you have been outside and give it a little grease or some drops of oil. This does not take long, and you will have a knife that will keep its new condition for a long time.

You can use regular shoe polish (the creamy kind) to make the leather shiny. A small amount of black shoe polish on brown leather gives a beautiful color that resembles antique-treated leather. For light, vegetable-tanned leather, use clear shoe polish, but wait until the sheath is completely dry before you apply the polish. After a great deal of testing—with everything from bone grease to saddle leather grease—I now only use shoe polish.

GRINDING AND HONING

Grinding and honing make your knife an effective tool. Usually, you will not need to grind, since the blade is already ground when it is made. Only if you happen to damage the edge or have an old, worn knife will you need to grind it. Also, grind the knife if it has a very worn or damaged edge, or if the bevel

(the entire ground surface that was the blade when you purchased it) has become rounded instead of sharp (Fig. 1).

Purchased blades almost always come with a ground finish. Traditionally, manufactured blades are ground on rotating grindstones. The disadvantage of this is that the round grindstone causes the bevel to become concave. The larger the grindstone, the less concave the bevel. The concave shape makes the edge thinner and less durable, a disadvantage particularly with hard knife steel. Care must be taken so that the edge does not "burn," making it less hard.

Fig. 1

Rounded bevel must be ground so it is straight.

Damaged edge is ground off.

Bevel

Today, most manufacturers use sanding belts that provide completely even grinding with more steel left on the edge. Most of us probably can't afford a privately owned sanding belt. Instead, you can use something such as a water-cooled grindstone made of Gotland stone. Unfortunately, the old hand-cranked ones, while excellent, are difficult to find nowadays. Since the stones are large and the speed slow, it is easy to monitor your grinding.

If you are thinking about purchasing a grindstone, buy one with as large a stone as possible, or put an ad in the paper for one of the old hand-driven types. The new, motor-operated ones have the advantage of grinding automatically. They also have a *grinding jig*, which keeps the knife in the exact position to get a perfect bevel.

Grind an even bevel, one side at a time. Proper grinding will cause a raw edge to form along the entire edge that will need to be removed by honing. The bevel of a woodworking knife must be completely straight all the way out to the edge. The entire bevel supports the wood, which facilitates woodworking. Having the bevel continue all the way out to a very thin edge is an ancient way of grinding knives in

Nordic countries. It works well in very soft steel. In the worst case, it may begin to wear with hard stress.

Modern hard, alloy steel is more sensitive. Hard treatment can break small pieces off the edge, making the knife blunt. To avoid this, the edge of the blade must be ground at a certain angle (Fig. 2). The angle should be anywhere between 10° and 30°, depending on what the knife is used for and how hard the steel is. A smaller edge angle is good for cutting wood and other soft materials, but the edge is too weak for cutting harder material. It easily loses sharpness. Greater edge angles are needed for hunting and provide strong edges for butchering, because the knife comes

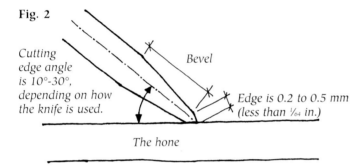

Fig. 2

Cutting edge angle is 10°-30°, depending on how the knife is used.

Bevel

Edge is 0.2 to 0.5 mm (less than 1/64 in.)

The hone

into contact with bone and cartilage. The same is true for work with very hard wood. When you try to whittle with a knife with a small edge angle, it will be sluggish. The blunt edge must work hard to get the shavings from the wood. Thus, you should have different kinds of knives to cover a wide range of tasks. Otherwise, you will eternally grind and hone. It takes knowledge and lots of practice to be able to grind well. Practice is the difference between success and failure, so practice as often as you can.

Honing takes place in a slightly different manner. When you hone, work only with the outermost part of the edge. How often it becomes necessary to hone depends, among other things, on the quality of the blade and how much the knife is used.

There are a large number of hones—made from anything from natural stone to artificial materials—that can be used today. In my childhood, sandstone and marble hones were commonly used (marble for

fine honing). The disadvantage was that they were quickly worn down and were too soft, even for a carbonized blade. On a blade made with today's hard, alloyed steel, you would practically wear down the entire stone to do any good.

Today hones are found in all degrees of coarseness, price classes, and sizes. Also, there is sharp, steel hone available that has a surface made of small, industrial diamonds. In my experience, these are the best hones; they hone the hardest steel quickly (without oil or other grease) and don't wear out.

An expensive, but excellent hone made of natural stone is the *Arkansas hone*. It is made of novaculite, a stone that is only found in one mountain in Arkansas in the United States. The stone is found in three degrees of coarseness. It is sawed directly out of the mountain, then ground down to various sizes and appearances. These stones are so long-lived that they will work for a lifetime. They come in three colors: the medium grade is gray speckled, the fine grade is white, and the extra fine grade is black. Do not forget that they are greased with thin mineral oil. Never use, for example, sewing machine oil—it only closes the pores and kills the effect! These hones should never be used completely dry. In addition, do not drop them on the floor. They break without fail. The ones attached to small wooden drawers or blocks are easiest to work with. Just attach them to a carpenter's bench, vise, or something similar. It is an unbelievable relief to have both hands free.

First, spread a heavy layer of honing oil on the hone. Place the knife flat against the stone. When

Fig. 3

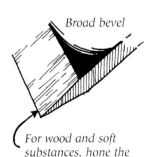

Narrow bevel

Broad bevel

Edge

For hunting and hard materials, hone an edge at a 10°-30° angle for a narrower bevel.

For wood and soft substances, hone the edge all the way to 0°.

Fig. 4 *Honing on the Arkansas hone from one direction.*

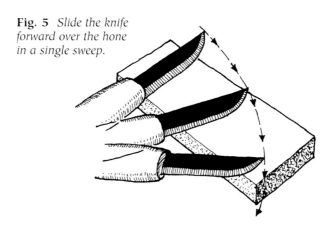

Fig. 5 *Slide the knife forward over the hone in a single sweep.*

Fig. 6 *Honing from the other direction at the same angle.*

Fig. 7 *A grinding support gives the proper honing angle.*

honing a knife for hunting, a 20° to 30° honing angle is sufficient (Fig. 3). Lift the back of the knife between 8 to 12 mm (⁵⁄₁₆ to ¹⁵⁄₃₂ inch) above the stone to get a honing angle of between 20° to 30°. About 8 mm (⁵⁄₁₆ inch) gives approximately 20°, and 12 mm (¹⁵⁄₃₂ inch) gives about 30°. Begin by using the small grinding support that comes with the stone; it gives 23° (see Fig. 7). Soon, you will be able to tell the correct angle without the grinding support. With the knife at the correct angle, slide the knife forward over the hone, and sort of cut a slice out of the hone every time (Fig. 4). Do it in a sweep (Fig. 5). Begin with the innermost part of the blade resting against the edge of the hone, then slide the blade away in a slight arc, so that the entire edge is ground. You will soon discover that the hone must not be too short. Turn the knife completely around after five or six strokes, and repeat the process toward yourself, always at the same angle

(Fig. 6). Press hard at first; reduce the number of strokes in each direction as you go, and reduce the pressure. Then change to the finer hone and repeat. This takes time, but don't give up! Wash off hones occasionally in lukewarm water and dishwashing detergent.

Rub the edge against a leather belt or newspaper. Rub with the edge backwards 20 to 30 times in the same direction on each side. This is called *strapping*. Now you can use the knife again. Grease the blade with a little oil, such as weapon oil, before putting the knife away.

You might want to carry a small pocket hone with you. Carbonized steel is particularly easy to hone. Hone along the edge with small circular movements, using the same honing angle as before. Hold the edge to the light to check your progress.

81

TWO PRACTICAL ACCESSORIES

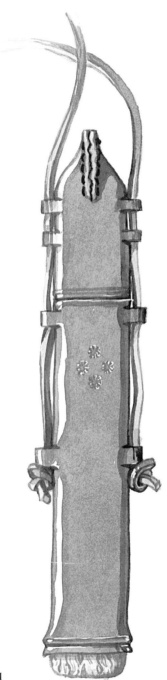

Fig. 1

T his section describes how to make two practical accessories: a case for a pocket hone and a case for a jackknife. Both the hone and the jackknife often go along to the woods, and it is nice to have them easily accessible. At the same time, cases reduce the risk of losing them. Refer to my models as sources for your own inspiration. Both work well, are easy to open and shut, and are simple to make. All that is needed is a small scrap left over from making a sheath.

POCKET HONE CASE

The hone case is made for a diamond hone (Fig. 1). The diamond hone is very effective, and you don't have to bring oil or grease with you. That's why it is one of my favorites. The case is made from bark-tanned rawhide, which keeps its shape and tolerates wear and tear.

Cut a wooden model to approximately the same measurements as the hone (Fig. 2). Add 2 to 3 mm (1/16 to 1/8 inch) to the length, width, and height. First, measure with paper approximately how much leather is needed, so that it can be sewed on the back side of the case. Cut the leather, let it sit at least 30 minutes in lukewarm water, then fold the leather around the wooden model and pull hard on the back side (Fig. 3).

Mark where the "tunnels" for the neck strap will go on the narrow side. Make eight pairs of parallel cuts, all just over 1 cm (3/8 inch) at the same height, straight across from each other on the narrow sides (see Fig. 3). This is easiest to do with a chisel. Divide the leather in a cover and a base section (Fig. 4). Put the leather in water again.

Make a little piece of wood for the bottom of the case in the correct shape, and hollow out a rim around the upper edge to attach the leather (Fig. 5). Wrap a wooden model of the hone with a couple of layers of plastic wrap. (Otherwise, you will not be able to get the model out when the leather has dried and shrunk.) Prepare two saddler's needles with pitch thread or similar thread. Take the leather for the base out of the water and wrap it around the lower part of the model, with the wooden bottom inserted (Fig. 6). Sew saddler's stitches on the back (Fig. 6), and press the leather for the rim, using something like the back of a knife (Fig. 7). Next, make the cover part (Fig. 8). Cut according to the pattern (Fig. 9), wrap it around the model, pull tight, and sew. When everything is in place on the model, it is time to make the holes in the tunnels. Carefully bend and stretch them out by slowly inserting a cone-shaped object through them,

such as a fat knitting needle or the handle of a water-color paintbrush (Fig. 10). Let them sit until the leather has dried.

JACKKNIFE CASE

A jackknife or pocket knife, for the most part, does not go well in a pocket at all. Almost all of them have sharp, pointed handles that quickly dig holes in the

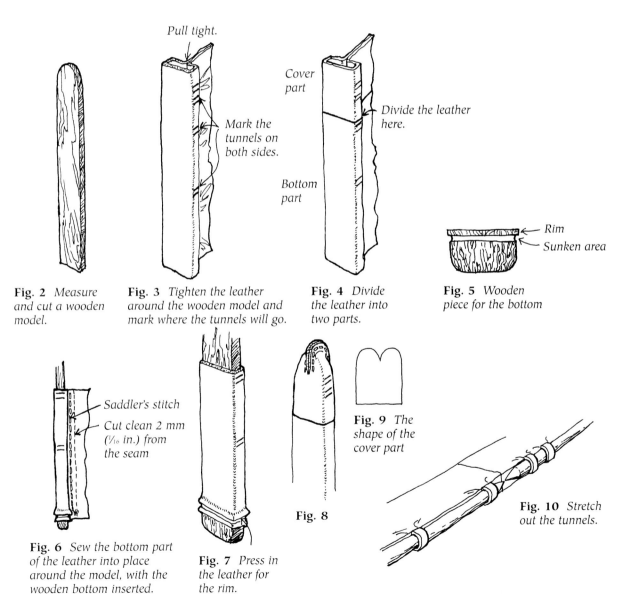

Pull tight.

Cover part

Mark the tunnels on both sides.

Divide the leather here.

Bottom part

Rim
Sunken area

Fig. 2 *Measure and cut a wooden model.*

Fig. 3 *Tighten the leather around the wooden model and mark where the tunnels will go.*

Fig. 4 *Divide the leather into two parts.*

Fig. 5 *Wooden piece for the bottom*

Saddler's stitch
Cut clean 2 mm (¹⁄₁₆ in.) from the seam

Fig. 9 *The shape of the cover part*

Fig. 8

Fig. 10 *Stretch out the tunnels.*

Fig. 6 *Sew the bottom part of the leather into place around the model, with the wooden bottom inserted.*

Fig. 7 *Press in the leather for the rim.*

83

pockets. In addition, they are too large. There are factory-made cases, but you will find they seldom fit your knife. In my experience, their hangers are also too stiff. This, combined with very coarse leather, means they often poke you in your back when you sit down.

My own case has a flexible, soft hanger that follows the movements of the body, and closes silently (Fig. 11). It is also easy to grab hold of the knife and to stuff it inside again without looking.

First, measure the dimensions of the knife. Make a corresponding indentation in some material that is exactly as thick as the depth of the knife. A piece of particle board or something similar works well (Fig. 12). The wood in the opening must be the same outer width as the case's exterior. Place a suitably large, softened piece of leather above this indentation. Press it down into the indentation, using a wooden

block that is exactly the same shape that you want the case (Fig. 13). How large should the piece of leather and the block be? Lets say that you use 2 mm ($\frac{1}{16}$ inch) thick leather. Then the block should be 4 mm ($\frac{5}{32}$ inch) narrower than the indentation (2 mm or $\frac{1}{16}$ inch on each side), so that there will be room to press the leather down. It doesn't make any difference how long it is, only that it is longer than your knife. Insert some paper first, to see how large the leather needs to be. Add extra for good measure.

Soften the leather really well, put it over the middle of the indentation, then press the wood block down through that area (Fig. 14). Begin furthest in and press outward. Take your time and allow the leather to find its new shape. Stretch hard! When the entire block is pressed down, fold the edges so that they lie flat against the area around the indentation.

Let it all sit under pressure for a couple of days until the leather has dried. After a day, you can remove the block so that the leather will dry throughout. The case will keep its shape.

Now you need to sew on the back piece, which ends in a lock on the front side (Fig. 15). Make a tunnel where the shaped wooden latch will be inserted (Fig. 16). Construct a hanger as depicted in Fig. 17, then rivet or sew the hanger to the back side of the case (Fig. 18). Add a small, leather strap for the latch to hang on, and make an air hole at the bottom. Finally, make notches on the front or on the sides to make it easier to get to the knife (Fig. 19).

Fig. 11

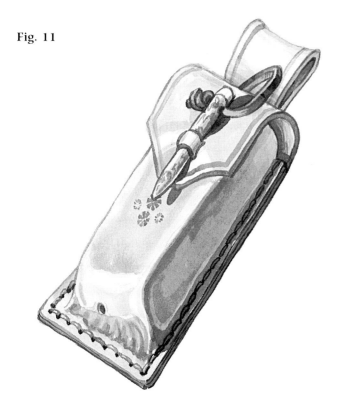

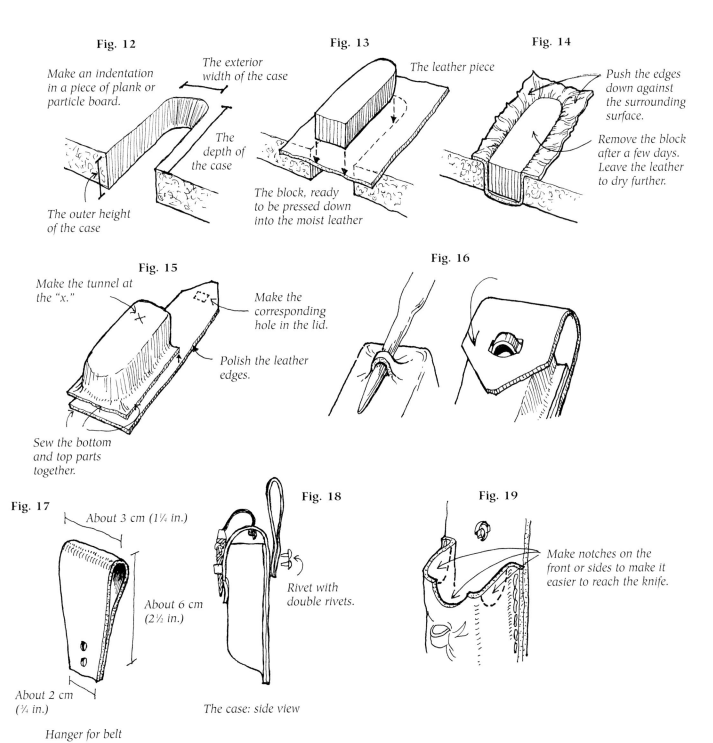

Fig. 12

Make an indentation in a piece of plank or particle board.

The exterior width of the case

The depth of the case

The outer height of the case

Fig. 13

The leather piece

The block, ready to be pressed down into the moist leather

Fig. 14

Push the edges down against the surrounding surface.

Remove the block after a few days. Leave the leather to dry further.

Fig. 15

Make the tunnel at the "x."

Make the corresponding hole in the lid.

Polish the leather edges.

Sew the bottom and top parts together.

Fig. 16

Fig. 17

About 3 cm (1¼ in.)

About 6 cm (2½ in.)

About 2 cm (¾ in.)

Hanger for belt

Fig. 18

Rivet with double rivets.

The case: side view

Fig. 19

Make notches on the front or sides to make it easier to reach the knife.

85

Carving knife (right) with sheath in curly grained birch (left). The handle is laminated from pieces of sallow, curly grained birch, Betula pubescens birch, and reindeer antler. The knife is fastened below the convex "wooden hat" at the top. The blade is short, pointy, and hand-forged in carbonized steel.

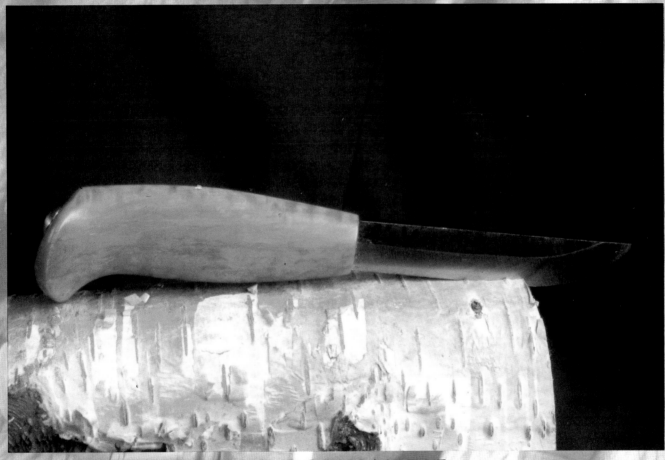

KNIFE WITH AN ALL-WOOD HANDLE
project on page 24

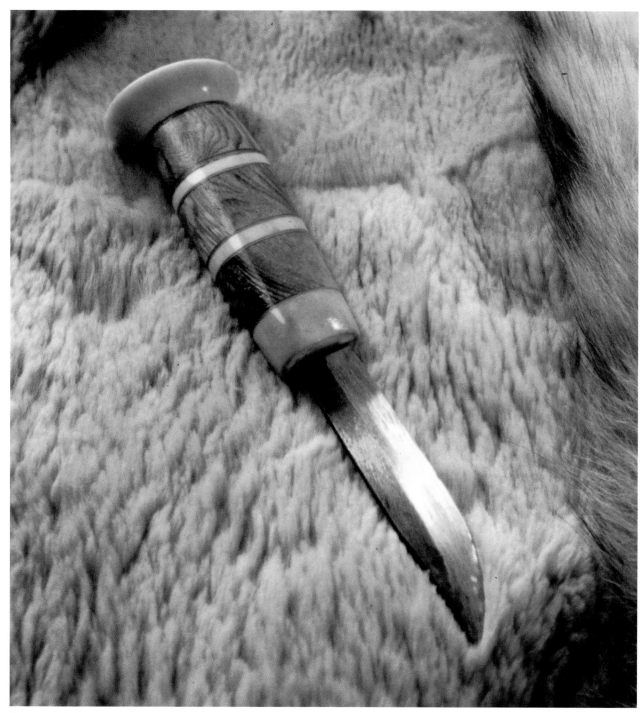

KNIFE WITH HANDLE
MADE OF MIXED MATERIALS

project on page 36

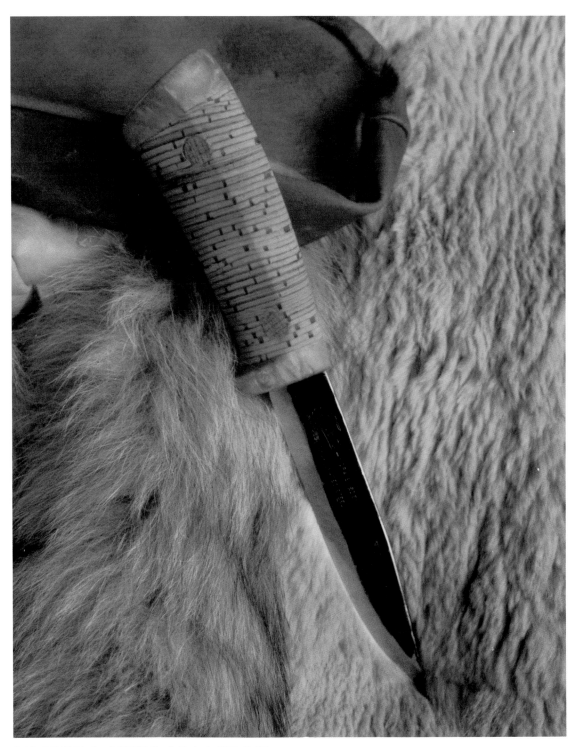

KNIFE WITH HANDLE
MADE OF BIRCH BARK

project on page 44

CLASSIC MULTIPURPOSE KNIFE

project on page 97

ROYAL KNIFE
project on page 106

MOUNTAINEER'S KNIFE
project on page 116

THE HÄLSINGE KNIFE

project on page 126

THE OLD TIMER
project on page 134

HUNTING AND FISHING KNIFE
project on page 140

PREHISTORIC KNIFE
project on page 146

CLASSIC MULTIPURPOSE KNIFE

This knife features a classic, simple spool-shaped handle. I consider this shape ideal, since I prefer a more subtle, less dramatic shape that is best suited for carving and woodworking. No matter how you grasp this classic handle, it feels just right, does not resist, has a good grip, and allows you to twist or turn the knife quickly.

At each end of this handle, there is a grouping of layers of metal, leather, horn, and birch bark. I position them there to get as strong and durable a knife as possible and to create the same effect as ferrules on other knives. Making the ends out of several different materials creates the impression of an engraved upper knife sheath. By making the ends alike, the knife acquires a harmonious, symmetrical appearance. These ends also frame the curly grained birch in the center. See the color photograph of this knife on page 90.

I have selected curly grained birch, because beautiful knives of this type are commonly made of this wood. It is also a very tough and resistant type of wood, and its surface can be sanded and polished to a great hardness and sheen. I selected the wood for the middle of the handle out of ten different pieces. When I glazed the wood later, I wanted curly grain with very tight whorls instead of a lot of "cat eyes." Despite putting so much work into the knife, I consider it a typical utilitarian knife. Though I based my selection of pieces for the middle on a great deal of experience, it is still always a guessing game. Not until the knife is finished will you know whether you have succeeded. Unfortunately, if everything doesn't go as planned, the only option is to start over and hope things go better next time.

Part of the charm of knifemaking is that the outcome is uncertain and the work is full of surprises. Sometimes I have the feeling that everything that could happen already has, only to have my mind changed a few days later. No matter how many knives I make, I learn something new from each one. Most of the time, it is something that was impossible

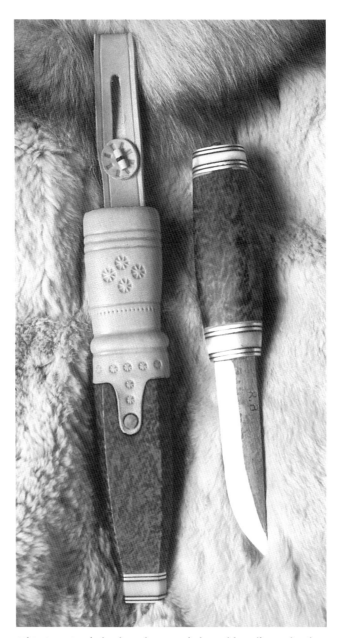

This is a simple knife with a spool-shaped handle made of curly grained birch. Metal, leather, horn, and birch bark wrapping make the simple design more interesting. The sheath, which is also of curly grained birch, has a leather upper section decorated with imprints of modeling irons and handmade stamps.

to predict from the beginning, no matter how well the work was prepared. I will leave it to you to judge how I have worked my way through these problems. I will list the requirements and hopes I had for each knife—and you can judge my success.

THE KNIFE

The first step is to check the knife tang. The ideal tang is one that is thickest where the blade enters the handle and gets narrower towards the back. Few blades look like this. The tangs of hand-forged blades vary a great deal. They are usually thickest where the tang is welded to the blade and become narrower along the blade. This is a problem for this knife. You want to achieve as exact a fit as possible between the first metal plate and the knife tang. If the fit is really good, the plate should not move sideways or up and down, because the stress on a knife is greatest at exactly that point.

If your blade has a welded joint, file it down as far as possible (Fig. 1). The part that is far up on the tang has hardened and can't be filed. But with a little luck, you can get the welded joint to be the same thickness as the blade attachment. The metal plate must attach to the blade as tightly as possible. To make a rectangular hole in the plate, drill two holes

Fig. 1 *Shape the tang with a file.*

that have slightly smaller diameters than the thickness of the tang and saw out the bridge between the holes. Then use files to gradually enlarge the hole until you reach the exact cross section of the tang. It is necessary to file for a while and keep testing it again and again. See Fig. 2.

The next parts to be installed should all have the same fit. The front (or top) parts of this handle are (in this order) metal, leather, metal, leather, horn, leather, metal, leather, metal and, next to the center piece, birch bark. The leather and the birch bark should be only .5 mm (¹¹/₆₄ inch) thick. You should be able to glue them into place at this point, but there may be a problem with the connection between the wood piece and the birch bark. Since it may require quite a bit of work, do not glue it yet.

You should have already decided which type of glue you will use. I used wood cement here. With this many pieces, I would not be able to mix, coat, and join with epoxy glue all the parts before they hardened, since it only takes about five minutes for epoxy glue to harden. So I waited to glue until after all the parts were made to fit together. Otherwise, it would take a week of gluing and drying until the handle was complete. See Fig. 3.

Next, measure and saw the wooden piece for the middle of the handle. Then sand the end surfaces of the piece completely flat, and determine with the slide caliper whether it is exactly the same length on all sides. Make a hole through this piece. The tang must go into and out of the exact center of both end surfaces. If this doesn't happen, the connection to the birch bark will be weak; it will be loose somewhere. You may have to saw out a new piece of wood and start over. As usual, two holes are drilled—one from each side, so that they meet in the middle of the piece. It is necessary to really concentrate, to not let your hand shake, and to rely on previous experience. The bridge between the holes is sawed out, then the hole itself is filed. It is a good idea to draw as many guide lines as possible before drilling, both above and below the side of the piece of wood (Fig. 4, page 100). Sight measurements are also helpful.

Assemble the pieces at the back end just as you did those at the front end, but in reverse order. The job of making rectangular holes in the parts of the back end progresses slowly. Find the midpoint of each piece, then sketch the height and width of the tang on them. Two holes are drilled, just as they were for the front end, and the bridge between them is removed. If the tang narrows towards the back, the hole must do the same (proportionally). A considerable number of parts will be used (Fig. 5).

Thread all the pieces and press them together. Next, measure how long the tang should be. In order to have room for a rivet washer, you will need about 5 mm ($\frac{11}{64}$ inch) of free tang. Usually, the end of the tang needs to fit through the hole in the rivet. Remove all the pieces, then saw or file until the tang has a rounded tip.

When the rivet washer is in place, the tang should only stick out a few millimeters ($\frac{1}{16}$ inch) from the hole in the washer, preferably less. Otherwise, the end of the tang will spread out too

Fig. 2 *The tang must fit the first metal piece exactly.*

much over the rivet washer after riveting. Try to achieve a durable knife with a very refined look.

Gradually, finish gluing the entire handle (Fig. 6). The glue between the parts increases the length of the handle a little bit, so I make sure that there is

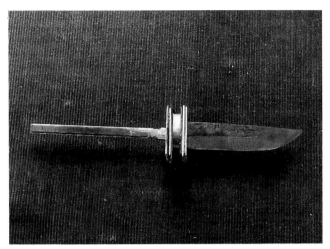

Fig. 3 *The front pieces are in place.*

a margin of about .5 millimeter ($\frac{1}{64}$ inch) behind the rivet washer. Then decide how much to compromise in gluing. All the parts except the last five or six are glued with wood cement. Use epoxy glue on the last ones, since you have time. It helps give extra strength to the back end. These parts have to attach themselves to the narrowest part of the tang. To further strengthen the back end, I drill a 4-mm ($\frac{5}{32}$-inch) oak dowel straight in from the back. This prevents the pieces from twisting around the tang.

As I mentioned, you have four to five minutes to rivet the handle before the glue hardens. It is necessary for all the pieces to fit, that none of them jam, and that you do not lose the rivet washer (which is taped into place). I rush over to the vise and tighten it around the blade, which is protected by pieces of wood. Tap on the end of the tang with the ball peen hammer quickly, since you may only have a couple of minutes left. The end of the tang will slowly begin to swell out over the rivet washer, pulling the whole handle together. Did you measure correctly? Did you add enough? At this point, there is no going back. If the riveting does not succeed, the knife doesn't succeed either. Twist the parts of the handle sideways to see if they stay in place and move less and less. How is the gluing? Note that it is beginning to harden. With a few final taps and some final tension and concentration, it is suddenly

Fig. 4 *The large piece for the middle of the handle with guide lines drawn on it.*

Fig. 5 *All the pieces for the handle, before they were threaded onto the tang*

all over. You can't do any more. The way the handle is joined together is the way it will stay. At this stage, the handle must dry and settle for a few days.

What you now have is a block that will gradually be shaped into a knife handle. The exact measurements have already been determined; in order to transfer them to the sides of the handle, the material must be somewhat smooth. Once the sides are roughly shaped, sketch the design on the handle. Then roughly shape the first two sides with a small coping saw (Fig. 7). (I have not succeeded in finding any other tool for this job.)

Very gradually, sink the saw blade down through the material. At this point, particularly when working with metal and horn parts, everything seems to come to a standstill. One side of the knife can take up to an hour to saw through—and then there are three

Fig. 6 *The handle is glued and riveted.*

Fig. 7 *The shape of the handle is sawed out.*

Fig. 8

Fig. 9 *The sides of the handle are filed.*

more. During this part, my thoughts often wander. I watch and don't watch what I am doing. My hand finds its own angle at which to hold the saw. Before I hang up the saw, an entire morning may be gone. My hand muscles and back ache, because of the uncomfortable working position. I have to straighten up and put down the saw; toward the end, I only manage to work five minutes at a time.

It's time to use the rasp and the file (Fig. 8). Begin to shape the roughly sawed sides with a rasp. The thousands of teeth in the tool will eat through the material. The pile of shavings grows endlessly. When the rasp has eaten its way down to the sketched-out contour lines, it is the file's turn to refine what the rasp has done (Fig. 9). You will produce a box shape that will become the handle, the outer contours of which follow those of the finished knife somewhat.

Next, round all the square edges. On a knife that contains so many materials, rounding the handle is a time-consuming procedure. It is necessary to work down through the corners to get the proper rounding. I begin by cutting the corners of the wood part first. The wood is very hard and cross-grained. As expected, it is very curly, wavy wood. Very small chips must be carved from the handle, and it is necessary to continually alternate between cutting towards and away from yourself. It is necessary to control the knife's movements. Too deep of a cut will split open some of the whorls in the wood. The cut may be so deep that it will never go away.

When one wooden corner is filed down, three more are waiting. The same cross-grained wood is everywhere. A file is needed to get rid of the horn and metal ends. The file goes down into the hard materials so slowly that it tests my patience. I look at the clock and calculate: almost a half hour per corner. Do not be discouraged—continue to use all the strength you can muster.

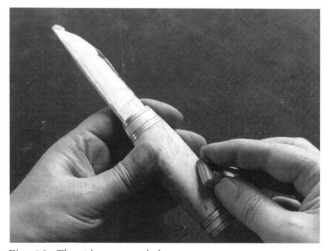

Fig. 10 *The sides are sanded.*

As the hours go by, the shape is revealed and begins to resemble a knife. Notice how much of the handle will be white horn, and how much will be colored. Will you succeed in keeping the gaps between the metal layers closed? At this point, I begin to feel certain that I can call it quits. There are

Fig. 11 *The hollowed-out area for the knife blade is made from the sheath material.*

Fig. 12 *The halves of the sheath are glued together under pressure.*

no loose parts. Measure with the slide caliper to make sure all the sides are the same length. Is there any deformity in the handle?

Yes, everything will probably succeed as long as you are careful and don't make any mistakes! This is the point at which you can begin to feel rewarded for all your efforts. The long, tiring hours are over for this knife and the workbench is full of scrap shavings. Yet this is just another beginning. Now more fun work begins. First, I check the blade and handle to make sure they are aligned. This can be best be seen by looking from the tip of the blade straight down along the blade and handle. They must form a completely straight line. At this point, it is too late to make corrections. There is simply not enough material left in the handle to correct it.

Next, begin sanding the handle with sandpaper, working from coarse to very fine sandpaper (Fig. 10, page 101); then move on to steel wool. Proceed with the process described earlier (see page 32): linseed oil mixture, polishing, and waxing.

THE SHEATH

The sheath for this knife is also made of curly grained birch. The outer shape of the sheath should be as similar to that of the handle as possible.

Therefore, it is important to find the right wood for the sheath. It should look as if both the handle and sheath were made from the same piece.

To avoid deviating from the shape too much, it is important that you have an exact sketch to follow. Make the sketch at full scale so that it can also be used as a pattern. Make the bottom part of the sheath with the same combination of materials that the ends of the handle are made of. But because you don't have a tang to build the sheath around, securely fastening the horn and metal parts may be a problem. Glue them with strong epoxy glue and insert two long screws for strength. The lower part of the sheath is subject to a great deal of poking by the knife.

You should have already selected some suitable wood. The sheath will be very rounded—like the handle—so an ample piece of wood is necessary. The leather upper sheath will go down a ways over the front side of the lower sheath, partly for decoration and partly to hold it in place. The leather that fits over the front of the sheath needs to fit in the same way an inlay does.

The first step is to divide the sheath material into two halves lengthwise. The most beautiful piece should be the front side. On the inside of each half, two hollowed-out areas need to be made for the

Fig. 13 *Wood and horn are glued and screwed to the bottom of the sheath.*

knife blade (Fig. 11). When marking the areas for the knife blade, a certain margin of space is needed. Otherwise, the knife may require extra coaxing every time it is inserted into the sheath.

Cut the contours of the hollowed-out area with a sharp knife, then hollow out the wood inside with a chisel. If you have selected a very cross-grained wood, you will have to continue alternating until you get down deep enough. You probably haven't considered how much effort it might take to complete this simple operation. Just to reach the bottom surface requires both sharp tools and patience, because the grain is wavy.

When both of the hollowed-out areas are ready, the surfaces of the halves need to be sanded until they are completely flat. The surfaces need to be examined carefully. Carelessness can cause gaps in the seams between the pieces. No matter how careful you are, obtaining a fine, nearly invisible seam is difficult. The ideal finished sheath looks as if it were made from one single piece. Saw apart the halves with as fine a saw blade as possible. Otherwise, there will be problems matching up the patterns in the wood.

Now you are to the point at which you join the halves together with wood glue (Fig. 12). Before you glue, test to see if the blade can be inserted easily

into the sheath and mark where the drain hole at the bottom needs to be drilled. Before pressing the glued halves together, check to make sure that both of the hollowed-out areas for the tip of the knife fit together exactly. Then press the parts together, steadily increasing the pressure until the glue begins to take. (Hold the pieces together as hard as you can for a couple of minutes before you squeeze them with bar clamps.) There is a risk that the halves will slip in relation to each other if the glue is too wet. Use as many clamps as you have room for to get as tight a seam as possible. Then put it aside and allow it to dry thoroughly. With a long, narrow drill bit, drill out a hole for the glue, which will eventually seep into the hollow space and crowd the blade.

When the glue has dried, the sheath has to be given its proper shape. It is just as important to have a pattern to work from as it was when you made the handle. Trace it as accurately as possible. First, sand the bottom of the sheath (where the metal-horn-combination will be attached) until it is flat.

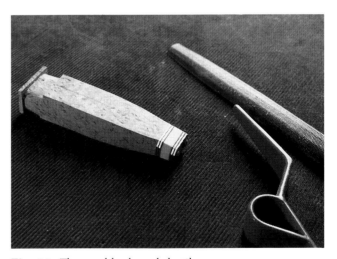

Fig. 14 *The roughly shaped sheath*

Make each piece of this metal-horn assembly separately to the same size, approximately 30 x 30 mm (1¼ x 1¼ inch). Then glue these together with epoxy glue. Allow the glue to harden for a few days so that it will have maximum strength. It's not suffi-

Fig. 15 *The model is positioned over the sheath and traced.*

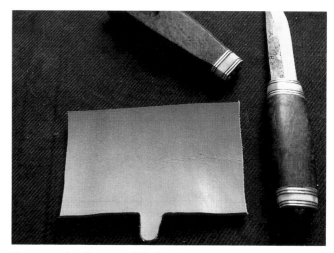

Fig. 17 *The shaping of the leather is complete.*

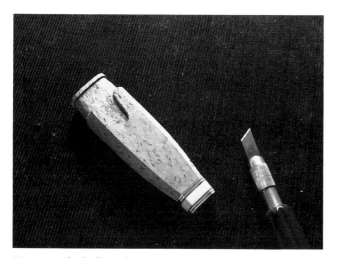

Fig. 16 *The hollowed-out area is complete.*

ished, use the rasp, the knife, and the file. Before going to sandpaper of various degrees of coarseness, begin to roughly shape the upper inlay recess for the leather. This entire area must countersunk to the same depth as the thickness of the leather (Fig. 14, page 103). You want the wood and leather surfaces to be flush. Leave a flange at the top, around which the leather will be molded to hold the upper sheath in place. Great caution is needed in working here, because the margins are so small. The walls should not be too thin. They should not be too thick either, because this would create too great a contrast in the transfer between knife and sheath. The leather in the upper sheath must also be roughly shaped.

When everything is ready, refine the sheath with sandpaper of various degrees of coarseness, the same way you did with the knife handle. When you are down to very fine sandpaper, stop to make the hollowed-out area in the front side of the sheath where the leather tongue will go. First, sketch and cut out a small cardboard pattern that looks the way you think the tongue should look, then transfer the pattern to the sheath (Fig. 15). Do a neat job with a hobby knife and chisel. The hollowed-out area must have the proper depth for a flush inlay (Fig. 16). Then proceed with the final surface treatment, as described for the handle (see page 102).

To finish, put the leather upper sheath into place. The cardboard pattern is needed now, because

cient to glue the piece directly to the bottom of the sheath. It will be too weak. There is no tang to attach it to here. Instead, insert two brass screws through the entire piece and a into the bottom of the sheath (Fig. 13, page 103). Thus, make sure that there is about 10 mm (⅜ inch) of substantial wood to screw into. The screws and contact surfaces are glued with epoxy glue and the piece is screwed tight. Then allow the piece to sit for a few days.

Just as with the handle, it is necessary to saw out the large outer contours of the sheath first. Begin sawing from the bottom upward. When this is finan appropriate piece of leather needs to be cut out (Fig. 17). Because the knife has a very oval handle, I do not dare to use shoe leather or Sami knife leather. It would be impossible to get the knife out when the leather dried. The other option is common vegetable-tanned leather, which stretches better. Sew the back seam with a saddler's stitch, leaving an "ear" to attach the hanger with a D-ring on the back side of the sheath.

When you have sewed the leather upper sheath into place, allow it to dry for a few hours before you decorate and dye it. (Decorating is always done before dyeing.) Next, make and attach the hanger. I have selected the type that is attached to the back side of the knife with a D-ring (Fig. 18). See page 74 for information on making this kind of hanger.

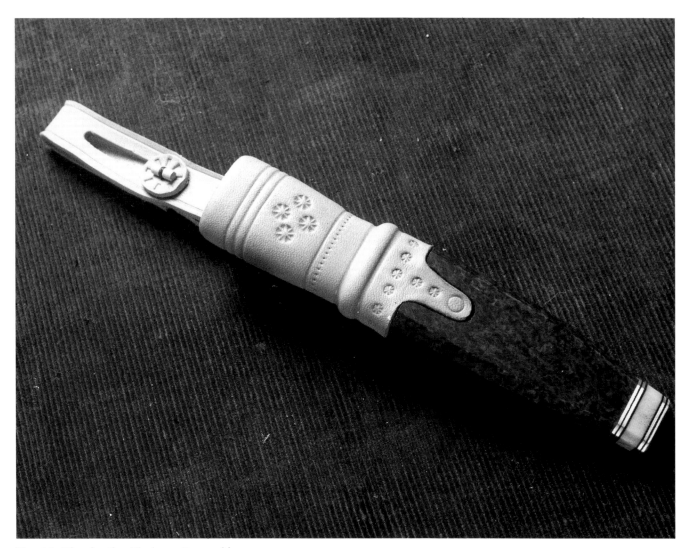

Fig. 18 *The sheath with decoration and hanger.*

105

ROYAL KNIFE

This is a powerful knife that is
strongly influenced by Viking
weapons and ornamentation. Despite
its complicated shape, it is practical
and easy to handle. Forged in one
piece by Heimo Roselli, the blade has
a shape that makes it versatile. The
sheath is made of birch, curly
grained birch, walnut, and reindeer
antler. The upper leather portion is
decorated with a triple braid and
stamped decorations.

The prototype for this knife was influenced by several sources. I wanted it to have elements from woodsmen and hunting knives, as well as from Sami knives. My intention was to try to create a knife that is as versatile as possible and, in terms of shape, a successful synthesis of all the finest knives I have seen in my life. I can't deny that the weapons and ornamentation of the Vikings have strongly influenced me. The roots of this knife go back 1,000–1,200 years, and are expressed in the Runic writing on the antler at the back end of the knife, and in the triangle with the symbol of eternity on the front of the sheath. Only a Viking could determine whether I successfully reached my goals.

The selection of blades was easy, since I wanted to make a heavy, powerful knife. It had to be broad, massive, and have an edge line with a wide radius, making it useful for everything, from carving wood to skinning wild game. I could either use Roselli's large hunting knife blade or another similar type of steel. Despite the blade's large size, it can be used for surprisingly fine tasks when you get used to it. This one has been decorated with carved wood and horn. See the color photograph on page 91.

In selecting the sheath, I tested my way—from all-leather sheaths to ones with an all-wooden lower part and a leather upper section. As you see, the latter won; it provided greater opportunities for expressive form, with heavier and more massive lines. As it turned out, it took quite a bit longer to make the sheath than it did to make the knife.

Happy circumstances allowed me to give one of the first knives of this model to King Carl Gustav. Despite its size, the knife has become somewhat of a favorite for me. I take it along on trips into the woods and fields. This has made it one of the most thoroughly tested knives of all the ones I have ever made. To date, I have not discovered any problems with it.

Because of the incredible amount of work required to make this knife, it is important to be careful when selecting materials and blades. If you have been saving really fine pieces, I suggest you use them for this knife. Also, try to find a blade that doesn't have too severe of an edge curve. This knife can be used for more than skinning.

Begin as usual, by examining the tang of the blade. If you have a Roselli blade, you will not have any blade problems, since it will have a welded, completely round tang. The hand-forged ones have to be filed first to achieve a blade that gets increasingly narrow from the blade toward the end. The first piece that needs to be fitted is the horn. Since the knife has a finger guard, it needs a very reliable piece. It might be hard to find such a coarse reindeer antler, so elk horn can be used instead. Even with thick reindeer antler, it is easy to run into marrow. This weakens the piece and has a negative impact on the appearance. As usual, be very careful fitting the front piece (Fig. 1). It has to absorb a great deal of force when the blade is used under stress.

Fig. 1 *The first piece set in place*

Next comes a layer of metal, then the large wooden handle piece. Try to fit all the pieces well. For safety's sake, use unworked pieces of handle material to allow some margin for error. Any excess can be removed later. Even though the back end of the knife gets a horn plate, rivet the knife at this stage of construction (Fig. 2).

As you can see in Fig. 3, you should shape the end of the tang with a file so that it will fit the rivet washer. Glue everything with epoxy glue and make

Fig. 2 *The handle is ready for riveting.*

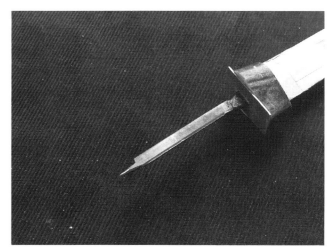

Fig. 3 *The tang end filed for riveting*

sure that the riveting really pulls the various pieces together. If done correctly, it will not be possible to dislocate the pieces in relation to each other. I don't use wood cement, because when I have taken apart older knives that were glued with wood cement, I discovered that the cement never dried properly inside the knife handle. Instead, the moist glue caused rust to form on the tang. You will not risk this when using epoxy glue. Even in an acid-free environment, the glue hardens chemically all the way to the tang. Epoxy glue also fills in all the hollow areas and strengthens the seams. In spite of its disadvantages, including the short hardening time, I prefer epoxy glue.

The riveted parts should sit and harden for a day. Make a cardboard pattern of the knife, then trace it on the side of the riveted parts. The knife's upper and lower sides can now be roughly sawed off, and rasped or filed into shape. On the upper and lower side of the handle, sketch out the midlines of the knife so that it is easy to determine how thick the handle is. Next, roughly saw the sides of the handle. Allow a rough margin for error, which can be corrected later. See Fig. 4.

Next, rasp and file down the various surfaces to get a perfect shape for the knife handle. It is useful to have a model for comparison. It is time to begin

whittling down the corners of the handle with a knife. Begin in the middle then move forward and backward toward the ends. Work on the oval back end as soon as possible. Sketch the outside shape

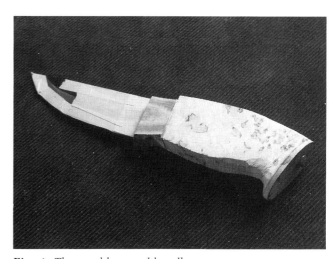

Fig. 4 *The roughly sawed handle*

then work your way down with a knife, rasp, and file. Finally, shape it as accurately as possible with sandpaper (Fig. 5). This is important, because otherwise it is impossible to make the outwardly curving back end. Make the outward curve very abrupt, so

Fig. 5 *The handle, roughly sanded and filed*

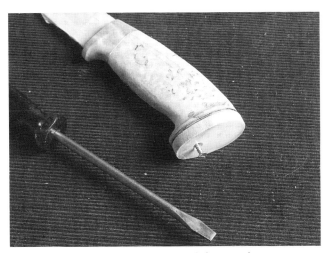

Fig. 6 *The horn plate is screwed tightly into place.*

that it will fit the hand well. Make the front end (with the finger guard) in the same way. Shape the outer contours first, then use round files to make the inward curves of the finger guard. Work your way as far down as possible to shape the entire handle. A file should hardly be needed afterwards. This method provides excellent control over what is happening with the handle.

When the back end is accurately shaped, it is time to begin on the back horn plate. To get a massive piece without marrow, the rosenkrans of an elk is used (page 12). It is sometimes hard to hand-saw an evenly thick piece. I rotate the piece and saw toward the center from all directions. Still, it is very difficult. Various corrections need to be made when the sawing is completed. Once the piece is sanded on both sides, a hollowed-out area must be made where the rivet washer can be hidden. I use a drill, a countersink, and a knife. The horn plate has to be screwed into the back end so it can sit properly. The screws need to be as far from the rivet washer as possible, so they can absorb force from twisting. Next, the excess pieces of the horn plate need to be sawed off as close to the oval back end as possible. Before the plate is glued and screwed into place, the horn plate and the back end must attach to each other as tightly as possible (Fig. 6). This is to reduce

the stress on the glued area. When everything is finished, allow the glue to harden for a day.

Next, finely sand the entire knife. Begin with relatively coarse sandpaper and work your way slowly down to very fine paper. Allow plenty of time for this, and don't hurry. All the sanding should be done under a bright light that offers good, moveable backlighting.

After all the sanding is complete, it is time to engrave the oval horn piece on the back end. On this particular knife, I carved the text in some old, runic symbols. Engraving is a chapter in itself, and I am definitely no specialist in the area. It requires almost daily practice. I use a slightly easier type that is not so hard to master. Nevertheless, engraving in hard elk horn is no easy job. It helps to moisten the horn a little. The technique is a little tricky, because you need to work with both hands at the same time. Hold the engraving knife in your right hand, so that only the bottom part of the tip of the knife sticks out between your thumb and pointer finger (Fig. 7). Engraving knives have a particularly sharp tip. Hold the handle in your left hand, and use the thumb of the left hand to press the tip of the knife forward through the horn, while the right hand controls the engraving knife, pushing it straight forward or in waves. Off and on, you will run into harder parts of the horn where it is not possible to push the tip forward, and you will need to rock forward with very small lateral movements.

Straight lines must be made in two steps. First, cut straight down in one direction. Then turn the object, and use the tip of the knife to make a parallel cut in the first line. The knife has to lean somewhat, so that the strip of horn between the lines comes loose. When this is done correctly, the strip curls in front of the tip of the knife the entire way. Do not press too hard or the tip will make scratches in different directions or the lines will be way too thick. If you get a sore thumb from this job, wrap the back of the carving knife with several layers of masking tape.

Sketch what you are going to engrave on the surface of the horn with a pencil (Fig. 8). This pencil sketch can be retraced often during this process, because it can be easily wiped off with your finger. What matters is that the knife finds its way along. Different kinds of hard steel work in various ways on horn. Some are almost impossible to use. The tip of the engraving knife must be newly honed. Test it on your thumbnail. Hold the tip at about a 45° angle, leaning toward the nail. It should immediately cut firmly into the nail. I check the sharpness of the tip throughout the entire job, and hone again as soon as it seems to be dull.

You can either engrave the entire pattern at once, or do it in steps and color afterwards. The advantage of the latter method is that you have control over what you are doing. For coloring, I use a finely ground powder, consisting of a mixture of alder bark and charcoal. Simply mix the powder with saliva. Linseed oil also works well. Use a finger to stroke the mixture over the engraving, then dry off the excess with a rag. If you sand the horn afterward, color it again.

I would advise practicing on sanded scraps of horn before engraving finished objects. A small mistake or wrong engraving can be repaired only if the horn surface is sanded all over again. And you don't have that kind of margin for error on a finished knife.

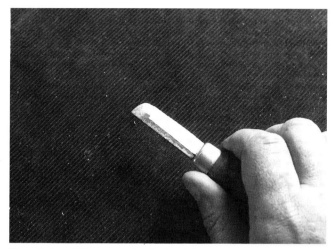

Fig. 7 *Hold the engraving knife this way.*

When the engraving is finished, shape and polish the convex wooden cap at the very back of the knife handle. Take a piece of wood that is large enough to completely cover the back end, then

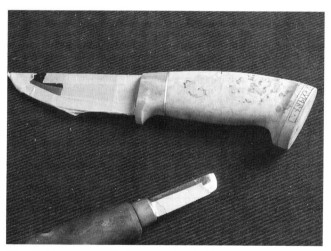

Fig. 8 *Make a pencil sketch on the knife handle.*

sketch the oval shape onto it. The convex cap needs to be the same shape, only on a slightly smaller scale. (This is a short cut to finding the shape, otherwise you have to try many times before you

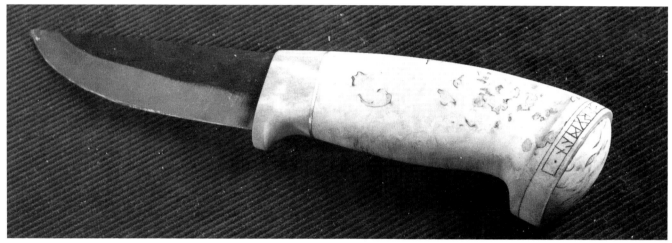

Fig. 9 *The finished knife*

succeed.) Then saw out your piece and give it a convex shape—first with a knife, then with a sanding block and various grades of sandpaper. It must be as finely sanded as the rest of the knife. Because it will not be subjected to great stress, it is then glued into place with epoxy glue.

Now the knife is mainly ready. What remains is fine tuning: water-polishing with steel wool, the closing of pores, and, finally, oiling (see the earlier section on finishing, page 32). See Fig. 9.

THE SHEATH

The sheath requires a little more work than the knife. Just as with the knife, use high-quality materials. The front side is built in sections of various types of wood, and the back side consists of a solid piece of wood to make the knife as strong as possible. If both the front and back sides are made of several small pieces, the risk for breakage increases.

Begin with the front side of the lower sheath, and build it from the top down. Use a paper pattern for the sheath, from which you will construct the entire front side. Then you can easily check to make sure that the pieces will suffice. At the top, have a piece of regular birch that extends down a little below the

lower edge of where the leather upper part of the sheath will be attached. It is important for it to be thick enough. Make the next piece out of curly grained birch. The contact surfaces between them should be sanded carefully, then glued with wood cement. Then comes a thin piece of birch, a piece of curly grained birch, a thin piece of birch, another piece of curly grained birch, and, at the very bottom a piece of horn, which won't be installed yet (Fig. 10). The fit between the pieces must be perfect; otherwise, the joints will be visible. All the pieces should be glued to each other while the handle is lying on a flat surface, so that the lower side will be completely flat.

When you have assembled the entire front side, turn it over and sketch the hollowed-out area for the blade on the back side. This is also the time to use a knife and chisel to carve the hollowed-out area (Fig. 11). This is much easier to do while the front side has a somewhat square shape, allowing it to be clamped properly to the workbench.

When the hollowed-out area for the blade has been made, it is time to shape the exterior of the front side. The pattern comes in handy for this job. The outer edges of the sheath must be ground to a very even shape so that they can be surrounded by a walnut frame. This step requires great accuracy. In order to perfectly fit the edge of the sheath, the frame pieces must have exactly the same shape. It may take an hour of sanding and fitting to produce each piece of the frame. Hold the work up to bright light to check that there are no gaps.

Next, glue the frame pieces into place—one at a time—to the edges of the sheath (Fig. 12). While they are drying, use bar-clamps to hold them in place.

Use rectangular pieces of walnut to make the edges. By making only one side of each piece into a frame at a time, you can use bar-clamps to hold each piece in place while gluing. Once the glue is dry, saw off the excess walnut and give the frame pieces a somewhat final outer shape.

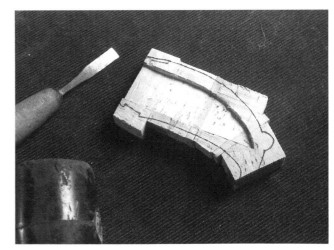

Fig. 11 *The hollowed-out area for the blade is ready.*

Fig. 10 *The beginning of the sheath*

Fig. 12 *The frame is glued into place.*

Saw the back side of the sheath out of a piece of birch (Fig. 13). (The wood must be long enough for the entire length of the sheath.) Lay the completed front side of the sheath against the wood for the back side, and trace the outer contours. Then trace the hollowed-out area for the blade on the wood for the back side as well and cut it out at a suitable depth. By holding the sheath halves against each other and looking from above, you can see whether the hollowed-out areas really match. If they don't,

make corrections. When you cut the hollowed-out area into the front piece, work slowly. Otherwise, there is the risk that the various pieces that make up the front side may break apart from each other.

Once the hollowed-out areas of both halves fit together, exactly, trace the shape of the front half on to the back half, then saw the back half with a coping saw. The sheath is ready to be glued together (see Fig. 15, page 114). But first, contact surfaces need to be sanded completely flat so that the best possible fit is achieved. Attach a rough piece of sandpaper to a flat surface and sand. (This method is least likely to give an uneven surface.)

Next, glue the halves together with wood cement. They should be held together with bar-clamps while drying (see Fig. 14). Fit and glue the horn piece furthest down on the sheath tip.

Once it is dry, you will have a very rough sheath that needs to be shaped (Fig. 16, page 114). Since the sheath has a very complex shape, begin with the big surfaces. First, do the front side of the sheath, shaping with a knife, rasp, and file, but sometimes first with a coping saw. Then it is time to shape the hollowed-out and inwardly curving shapes on the front side, which are removed with a gouge (Fig. 17, page 114). Finally, use round files of various sizes, among other things, to shape all the convex and concave areas.

Once the front side is roughly shaped, shape the back side of the sheath. Its appearance will vary from knife to knife. Sometimes I make a simple, flat

Fig. 13 *The material for the back side of the sheath is sawed out.*

Fig. 14

back side. Other times, I carve out concave areas on the back to give it a sort of wavy pattern. It all depends on what you feel like and what you think fits. I usually make the back side of all of my wooden

sheaths completely different from the front side.

Sanding the exterior is the next step. For such boldly shaped sheaths, begin with very coarse sandpaper and move down in coarseness as you go. Sand the whole sheath with one thickness at a time. When you get to very fine paper, it is time to begin to think about engraving the front side of the sheath (see Fig. 18, page 115). It consists of an upper section that has engraving directly on the sheath's surface, and a triangle decoration that I carved from a piece of horn after brushing it off and polishing it properly. The decorative piece is sawed out of the piece of horn, and its edges are beveled inward somewhat and put in the correct position on the sheath. Then, trace around the piece. Using a knife and a chisel, make an indentation in the sheath that is as deep as the piece of horn is thick. If the hollowed-out area is too tight, sand the edges of the horn pieces somewhat. When the blade can almost be pushed inside, the glue is applied to both surfaces, and a bar-clamp is used to press the horn piece the rest of the way down.

The remaining jobs are completing the wooden part of the sheath, polishing it with steel wool (after raising with water), closing pores, and, finally, oiling.

Fig. 15 *Both halves of the sheath are ready to be glued together.*

Fig. 16 *The front side of the sheath, roughly shaped*

See page 32 for finishing instructions.

Next, the leather upper part needs to be fit and sewed. First, measure the height of the leather piece. It needs to reach from the inlay on the sheath part, to above the thickest part of the handle. This piece needs to be wide enough to wrap around the knife. Sew the back seam with a saddler's stitch, leaving a long "ear" for both a D-ring and a belt slot (Fig. 19).

On the front side of the leather upper sheath, position a small triple braid that fits exactly into the middle of the leather. (This technique is described in the next project, page 124.) First, make two rectangular holes with the help of a hollow punch and a chisel. Stick the two ends of the braid through these holes and glue them to the back side with contact adhesive. When all the preparations are complete, the leather piece should be softened.

Because the knife has a finger guard, you will need to wrap the handle in a layer of plastic wrap, then fill in the cavity between the finger guard and the thickest part of the handle with modeling clay. (This filler should not go outside the outer contours of the handle.) When the modeling clay is fit into place, wrap a layer of paper and another layer of plastic wrap around it. The handle is now completely protected against moisture. It's time to insert the knife in the sheath and begin sewing the handle into

Fig. 17 *The front side, roughly cut out*

place. Once everything is ready, the knife should dry for two days.

When the knife has dried four to six hours, you can make the decorations on the front side of the upper sheath. This can be repeated several times. It is particularly important to press the leather around the flange at the top of the lower sheath so that the upper sheath will remain tight.

When the upper sheath has completely dried, it should be trimmed on the back side. Then make the horn-rivet, which is placed on the lower part of the upper sheath. Its purpose is to help hold the upper sheath in place. I make it about 6 mm (¹⁵⁄₆₄ inch) in diameter, and a few centimeters (about ¾ inch) long.

Because it will extend into the lower part of the sheath, a corresponding hole must be made. This has to be done carefully so that you don't drill into the space for the blade. Once the horn-rivet fits into the hole, it should be glued and tapped into place with a rubber mallet.

Fig. 18 *The engraving is ready to be transferred to the front part of the lower sheath.*

When everything is in place, it is a good time to color the upper sheath with grain blacking in an appropriate color, if you wish.

Next, make the hanger. It is made as a triple braid (see the next project, page 124) and hung by the ear of the back side of the knife with the help of a D-ring (see Fig. 19). Position the D-ring by making a hole in the ear first, tightening up the D-ring somewhat, threading it into place on the hole, and, finally, clamping it together again with pliers. Note that the triple-braided hanger needs to be colored before it is braided together.

When everything is in place and has dried, the leather must be greased with several applications of leather grease, then, to achieve additional shine, polished with cream shoe polish. Finally, all the edges are colored with black grain blacking. The upper sheath is also colored black on the inside as far down as you can reach. When the upper sheath has dried, the inside should be coated with a layer of plastic lacquer to stiffen it further, if so desired.

Now the knife is essentially finished, so the blackened edges can be polished with beeswax (Fig. 20).

Fig. 19 *The hanger with the D-ring*

Fig. 20 *The finished sheath*

MOUNTAINEER'S KNIFE

T he shape of this knife is entirely my own. I wanted to further develop the royal knife (see page 106). First, I wanted a real finger guard. It was not only to be a broad hilt, but also accommodate the rounding of the finger farthest down. There should be proper protection on the sides. At the back, I wanted to have the pointer finger properly anchored through an indentation on the bottom side of the knife. In Norwegian fashion, the handle was to be widest at the top, and narrow toward the bottom. This would allow the little finger to reach all the way around. I also shaped the back end so that my hand wouldn't slide backwards when doing hard work. The result is a knife with a slightly unusual shape. It is mainly created with hunting in mind, and is definitely not a carving knife. The shape of the blade makes the knife useful in both butchering and skinning.

There were a few problems creating the sheath for this knife. First I made a conventional all-leather sheath. Even though it worked well, I did not think it did justice to the knife. Finally, I chose a sheath with a wooden lower part, just like the previous knife (page 106). The leather upper part had to be made so that it could be opened around the low finger guard. I had to test the upper part with several paper models to determine its shape. The trick was to find a shape that made it easy to insert and remove the knife from the sheath.

Several times I was close to giving up. For the sake of simplicity, I tried putting the seam of the upper sheath on its side and fastened the hanger directly through the indentation in the upper sheath. This arrangement allowed the knife handle to fit neatly into the upper sheath. It was necessary to consider this when adding the snap. The hanger is an adjustable length of triple braid. Of all my knives, this is the one that takes the longest to make. Be sure to make the knife first. For a color photograph of this knife, see page 92.

This knife has a handle that narrows towards the back, with a strong finger guard that provides a firm grip. The bottom half of the sheath is made of curly grained birch, birch, walnut, juniper, and reindeer antler. The leather upper sheath can be opened at the side to allow room for the finger guard. The hanger is braided, and its length is adjustable.

116

THE KNIFE

The piece of horn closest to the blade must be taken from a really hearty piece of horn. Usually, the only way is to use the piece closest to the rosenkrans on a strong elk's antler (see page 12). It is also necessary to select a piece with as little marrow as possible. The hole for the tang should be drilled from both directions so that they are at right angles to the piece of horn. As before, the hole must fit tightly around the tang (Fig. 1).

The next step is to shape the front side of the finger guard against the blade (Fig. 2). First, shape the finger guard's curve downward. This should be done as accurately as possible. File the front surface to the proper shape. Then sand it, using all grades of sandpaper until the front surface is completely shiny and without scratches. Do this before you glue the piece into place. With the blade in place, it is much more difficult to reach. If you should get a somewhat loose fit in the blade attachment when the first piece of horn is glued, wipe off all the glue that comes out where the blade is attached.

There may be a gap between the blade and the horn piece. If so, mix a small batch of epoxy glue; stir in a small amount of sanded powder from the horn to make it a very thick mixture. Use this to fill the gap so that there are no openings where the blade is attached. The front side of the piece of horn should be completely wrapped with masking tape, except for the opening around the blade itself. When the glue has hardened, it is not possible to patch the solid horn. I use a carpenter's square to make sure that the tang goes into the first piece of horn at a right angle, both vertically and horizontally. All glue has to harden for at least a day.

I selected curly grained birch for the wooden piece in the middle. A pattern of the knife is helpful in making it fit. This can be placed on top of the wooden piece to check that there is enough room for everything. Use a good-sized piece of curly grained birch so that you have extra margins.

There is a thin intermediate layer of leather between the wood and the horn. To get good seams,

make sure that the fit between the horn and the wood is correct before inserting the layer of leather. Leather has the ability to absorb uneven areas, but is visible when the finished knife is rotated on its axis. The back end of the wooden piece needs to be sanded completely flat before the piece can be glued (Fig. 3). It can't be reached once the tang is sticking out through it.

Fig. 1 *The piece for the upper part of the handle is fit into place.*

Next, saw off the rear horn piece. The sawed surfaces are then sanded completely flat. Use the slide caliper to make sure that the bottom edge of the piece has an even thickness. If this piece is completely without marrow, it is a good idea to rivet it directly to the horn. If not, the end of the tang has to be sanded so that a rivet washer can be used instead. Do the riveting at this point, then hide the rivet head underneath a round cap at the end. Glue the piece in the middle with epoxy glue.

After the handle has dried for a few days, it is time to begin roughly sawing it (Fig. 4). The pattern is used to trace the outline of the handle onto the side of the material for the handle. I usually start by sawing off the upper and lower parts. Then these parts are rasped and filed down to where the line was sketched. Next, the longitudinal sides of the handle are sawed out. (Use sketched lines to help

Fig. 2 *Round the first piece of handle on the bottom edge.*

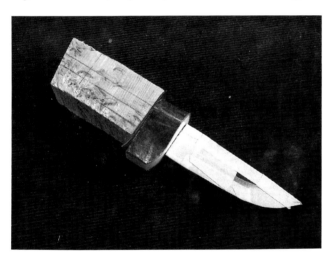

Fig. 3 *The wooden piece in the middle of the handle is glued into place.*

Fig. 4 *The handle is roughly sawed.*

back end of the horn piece with a rasp and file. To reduce the slow sandpapering job as much as possible, saw out as much detail as you can (see Fig. 5). Once the handle has been shaped, move on to sandpaper. As usual, it is a matter of working, step-by-step, through many degrees of coarseness of sandpaper until the handle is completely free of scratches and has a silky finish.

Now make the rounded button for the end of the handle. Use a piece of curly grained birch that is rectangular in shape and so large that it covers the whole round rear piece of horn. Mark this shape on the piece of wood. If you follow the shape exactly, you can get the shape of the cap on a smaller scale. When it is marked, hack around it with a knife until

you saw these as well.) See Fig. 5.

Now it is time to round out the shape of the handle. Use a knife for the wooden part; a rasp and a file for the horn parts (Fig. 6). Because of the curved shape of the finger guard, it can be difficult to reach at all angles. Thus, you will probably need to use a power drill with round and flat attachments (Fig. 7). In order to reach all the difficult and tight angles, finish by using a smaller drill with very small tips. On the other hand, it is possible to shape the

you get an even, rounded shape. Then take a sanding block and work on the shape some more. When it begins to look good and feel right, it is time to sand the cap in the same manner that you did the handle. The sanding must be complete before the cap can be mounted.

Make a notch for the rivet washer on the back side of the cap. Also, drill a hole for a screw that will pull the cap to the knife. The head of the screw is countersunk into the cap. The only thing that remains is to glue with epoxy and pull the button tightly into place. The handle should now be ready for the final surface treatment. See page 32 for finishing instructions.

As you can see from the photos on pages 92 (color) and 116, I have decorated my handle by drilling and gluing round dowels. Whether you do this is a minor matter. However, the round dowels must already be drilled into place when the rough shaping of the handle begins. This is so that there will be a margin to sand off any splinters that may be created by the drilling.

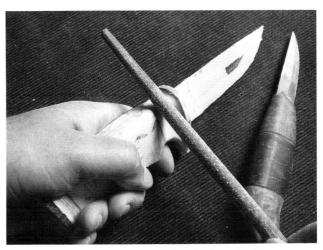
Fig. 6 *The handle is shaped with a knife and a file.*

Fig. 5 *The roughly shaped handle*

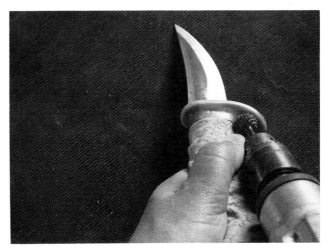
Fig. 7 *It may be necessary to grind out certain parts.*

THE SHEATH

Make this knife sheath in sections, beginning at the top with a piece of really light birch. It should reach down about 1 cm (⅜ inch) below the edge of the leather upper sheath to create a nice contrast. Use patterns to make the sheath just as you did with the handle (Fig. 8). One pattern will reach out to the sheath's frame—that is, cover the curly grained section. Another pattern will cover the whole sheath. If you don't have a whole piece of curly grained birch, the front side can be built up in sections, moving downward. It is a matter of finding a piece of curly grained birch with a good grain, since so little of it will be seen on the finished sheath. Once the front side is complete, make a sketch on the back side to show where the hollowed-out area for the blade will go.

Cut out the contours of the blade with a sharp knife, then hollow out the area with a chisel. It is important to do this while there is still an opportunity to clamp the piece to the bench (Fig. 9).

Once this is done, use the inner pattern to trace the basic shape of the sheath, then saw out the shape with a coping saw (Fig. 10). Once this is done, all the sawed surfaces need to be shaped. This can be quite a tricky job. The surfaces of the sides must be completely flat. In addition, the shape needs to be completely even lengthwise. The most difficult part is evening out the surfaces in the crosswise direction. It is easy to create a somewhat rounded groove with a file, a sanding block, and sandpaper. Therefore, it is a good idea to alternately sand lengthwise and crosswise.

When this has been completed, it is time to frame the curly grained birch section. Either horn or wood can be used for the frame. (It is easier to make the wood look nice.) The frame pieces on each side are sawed from rectangular wooden planks of a suitable thickness. Place each wooden plank under the sheath and trace the contours. The frame pieces must be sawed with the greatest precision. The more precisely you saw, the less work there will be afterwards. The sawed section needs to be perpendicular to the surface of the frame piece. Work on one side of the sheath at a time.

Next, sand the sawed surface so that you get a perfect fit between the sheath and the frame. Work carefully here. Sand off tiny pieces of the frame until there is a good fit along the entire length of the frame. Alternately sanding the surfaces of the sheath and the frame works just as well. To get the greatest durability, glue and screw the frame pieces. The frame pieces are glued in one at a time (Figs. 11 and 12). Tighten them with bar-clamps or, when this will not work, with leather straps, shoe laces, or something similar.

When everything is ready, it is time to begin shaping the sheath (Fig. 13, page 122). Always begin by deciding what the profile of the sheath will be. The contours of the sheath form an arch, with the lowest point in the middle and the highest points furthest up and at the tip. The next step will be to shape the sides of the sheath. From a slight longitudinal "back" in the center, thin out the shape

Fig. 8 *The sheath is built with the help of patterns.*

Fig. 9 *The hollowed-out area for the blade is made.*

toward the edges.

Then it is time to shape the back side. Make it from a whole piece of wood; this is important, since it braces and strengthens the front side (which is made in sections). Place the front side against the material for the back side, and trace the outer edges. The hollowed-out area for the blade must now be made the same way it was for the front side (see Fig. 9, above). Make a good-sized hollow area so that the knife will not get stuck. When the hollowed-out area is ready, the contours are sawed, according to the lines that were drawn on it. It will soon be time to glue both halves together. But first, the contact surfaces have to be sanded down so that they are perfectly flat. It is easy to have gaps at the tip of the sheath. When the halves are glued together, it is important to make sure

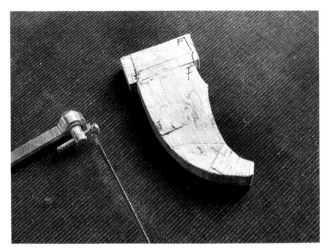

Fig. 10 *The rough shape of the sheath is sawed out.*

that the blade tips in the hollowed-out areas match each other exactly. Then the sections are joined together with several bar-clamps and allowed to dry, making any rough adjustments of the outer contours of the sheath so that the edge will be even. Now is a good time to make a final decision on how wide the frames will be. The front side is roughly shaped (see Fig. 13, page 122).

It is now the back side's turn. Its surface can be shaped according to taste, either as a very smooth or a more elaborate surface. Make a flange on the upper part of the lower sheath so that the leather upper part can grab on to it. The leather upper part is recessed into the wooden surface of the sheath, so that the finished sheath will have a completely flush outer contour.

There will be a horn end and a final cap at the tip of the sheath, which should now be put in place. Reinforce the gluing at the horn end by pounding pieces of thick steel thread in predrilled holes, or by screwing the horn piece into the sheath with two

screws. Once the glue has dried, give the horn piece its proper shape. Finally, attach the cap (which can be made in curly grained birch for the sake of contrast). It is screwed into the horn piece and into the sheath, and the head of the screw is countersunk.

When all pieces are in place, the sanding job begins. Begin sanding the whole sheath with coarse sandpaper and go down to increasingly fine sandpaper. When you reach very fine paper, it is time to begin thinking about the inlay. On this sheath, I have made an inlay from thin end pieces of juniper wood.

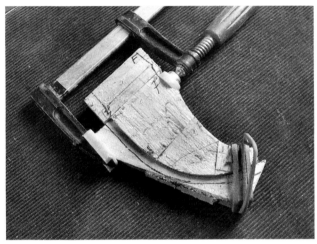

Fig. 11 *The first frame piece is glued.*

Fig. 12 *All the frame pieces are glued.*

121

Fig. 13 *The front side of the sheath, roughly shaped*

First, saw all the pieces straight down through the core (Fig. 14). Then cut them at right angles so that they will be large enough for inlay pieces. Then all the pieces are placed edge to edge, with a half-piece vertical displacement (Fig. 15). This will give you an interesting S-shape from each core, which winds through the entire inlay section.

Now the edges of all the pieces are sanded so that they will fit against each other properly. Then they are glued together in the proper order. When the glue has dried, give the inlay pieces their outer shape and sand them very evenly. Then the section needs a thin outer frame, which I made out of walnut in this sheath. When the frame needs to be fit, make it in the same manner as you did the outer frame.

Finally, the frame has to be sanded and trimmed down to the proper thickness. Now it is easy to trace the inlay section onto the front side of the sheath. Determine very exact measurements for how large a hollowed-out area you need to make. Before you trace the inlay section, give its sides a slightly inward-sloping shape. The hollowed-out area is made with a small knife and chisel. Of course, the bottom of the hollowed-out area must be completely flat. The bottom of the inlay section also needs to be sanded until completely flat.

Carefully adjust the whole sheath. It is necessary for all sides to fit tightly, particularly the tip. When the inlay section goes almost all the way down into the handle, glue and press it the rest of the way with bar-clamps. If everything has been done correctly, the fit should be good. NOTE: The inlay pieces should not be too thin. It should be possible to shape their upper surfaces to the slight "back" that the rest of the sheath has.

Once the glue has dried, it is a good idea to use a knife and file to give the inlay its proper outer shape. Finally, the surface of this section is sanded down with sandpaper so that it connects with the rest of the surface of the sheath.

To allow proper airing and draining, I drill a 3-mm (⅛-inch) hole in the bottom of the sheath and an air hole on each side of the sheath. The hole is then countersunk so that it will be neat.

When the sheath gets its final surface treatment with steel wool, water raising, pore closing, and so on, put it in a mixture of boiled linseed oil, turpentine, and paraffin oil for a few days.

Then make the leather upper sheath. For a knife with such a long finger guard, the sheath needs to be open on one side. I have designed my own pattern in which the leather overlaps and is snapped together with a strong snap. In order to find the proper shape of the leather, you will have to test your way along. Make extra wide margins in order to have room to cut it off where necessary. It may be a good idea to begin by using a piece of paper that is wrapped around the knife. It is important for the knife to be in the sheath the whole time you are testing.

The upper sheath has a small triple braid of thin leather, which is inserted through slits in the leather and glued to the back side. The triple braid is mounted before the leather is softened. In shaping the leather upper sheath, it is important to be able to easily insert and remove the knife from the sheath. This is the reason for the rounded corners. When the leather is moist, it is easier to shape around the handle of the knife. Note that before the knife is inserted in the sheath, it should be wrapped with plastic wrap to protect it from wet leather.

Fig. 14 *Juniper pieces used for inlaying*

are used. Once the leather has dried for a few hours, press the decorations in around the small triple braid (see photo on page 116).

The knife should remain in the sheath for a few days until the leather is completely dry. Then it is fine to dye the leather with grain blacking of a suitable color, if you wish. Dye all the visible leather edges with black grain blacking. Then rub beeswax into the leather and polish with a bone folder several times until the edge becomes really shiny. Once the grain blacking is dry, polish all the leather with leather grease. Repeat this several times. When you notice the leather is beginning to

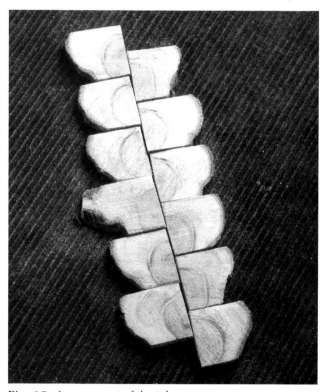

Fig. 15 *Arrangement of the inlay*

The leather is sewed together only along the small piece that surrounds the lower part of the sheath. The remainder of the upper sheath is one piece. It works well to measure out space for the snap after sewing. First, add the upper part of the snap. Then, by pushing it against the lower layer, get an exact marking of where the bottom part of the snap will be mounted. (Of course, the knife needs to be in the sheath.) The upper sheath attaches to a very small surface on the wooden part of the sheath. In order to keep it in place, make a rectangular raised area on the front part of the wooden portion of the sheath that the leather can grab. This is very important! Otherwise, it will not be possible to keep the upper sheath around the lower sheath. This raised area can be glued into place afterwards or be a part of the sheath itself.

While the leather is moist, it is easy to shape around the raised area. To further strengthen the attachment of the upper sheath, screw brass screws through the leather into the wood. Four such screws

look dry again, repeat as needed. Finally, polish the leather with creamy, uncolored shoe polish to achieve a shiny surface.

At this point, there are just a couple of things left to make. The first is the hanger. It is made from a triple braid, which also has a buckle to adjust the length. See Figs. 16 through 18.

TRIPLE BRAID

An inward triple braid must be braided in multiples of six—that is, braided 6 times, 12 times, 18 times, and so on. Follow the step-by-step photographs in Fig. 19 (page 125) and the instructions below.

A. Make two parallel cuts in the piece of leather.
B. First braid. Hold number 3 and place it under number 2. Work with the thumb and pointer finger of your right hand.
C. Second braid. Number 1 is placed under number 3. Go to the thumb and pointer finger of your left hand. This will leave the second strip free.
D. First turn. Keep number 1 below number 3 with your thumb and pointer finger. Find the loose number 2 with your right hand and turn it away from you, upward and toward yourself, between itself (the 2) and the 1.
E. Third braid. Put the 2 under the 1 with your right hand and pointer finger.
F. Fourth braid. With the thumb and pointer finger of your left hand, push the 3 under the 2.

G. Second turn. Keep your grip and let the 1 hang loose. Turn it the same way (away, up, toward yourself); but this time, the 1 hangs loose between the 2 and the 3.
H. Fifth braid. Using the usual grip with the right hand, take the 1 under the 3.
I. Sixth braid. Preform the same technique with the left hand: the 2 under the 1. Then start over from the first braid, if desired.

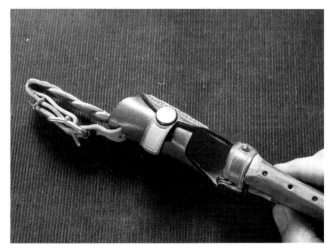

Fig. 17

Fig. 16 *The upper sheath from the front (Fig. 16), the side (Fig. 17), and the back (Fig. 18).*

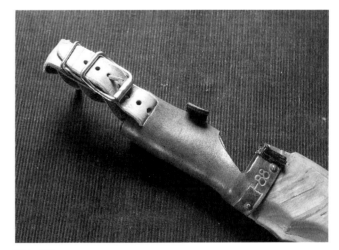

Fig. 18

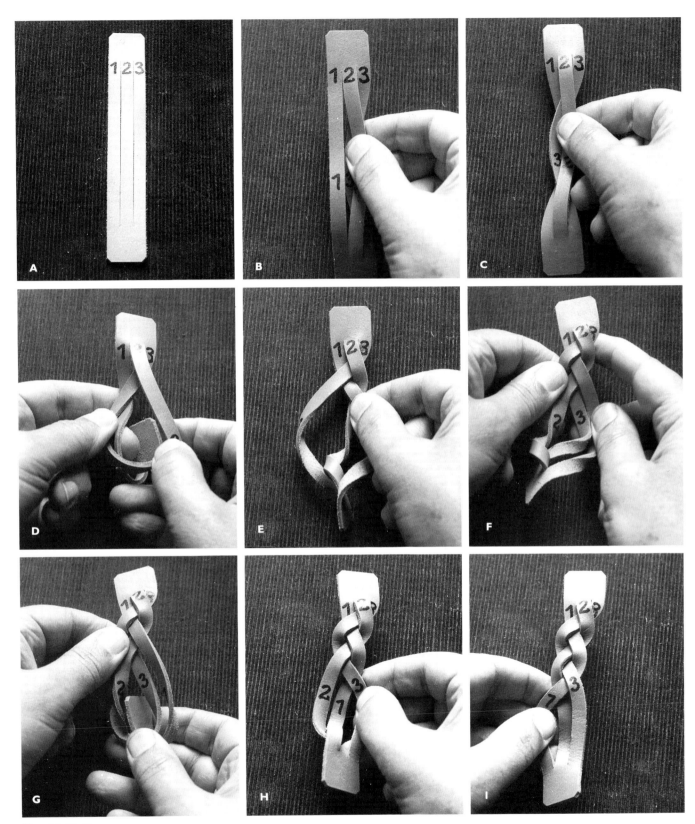

Fig. 19 (A-I)

THE HÄLSINGE KNIFE

This knife has a slightly unusual construction. Birch bark in the handle gives it a light and fine grip in all kinds of weather, and leather and horn increase its strength. The sheath is made from the same materials and requires a little patience from the knifemaker. The upper part of the sheath—made of Sami knife leather—has been decorated with modeling irons and stamps, and has an adjustable hanger.

I made this knife to enter into a knife competition in an area of Sweden that was looking for a knife to symbolize the district. See page 44 for instructions for making a simpler—but very similar—birch bark handle.

I had heard a lot of good things about knives made with birch bark handles. Indeed, birch bark offers a very good grip. It does not get slippery, even when wet. It's also nice to hold when it gets cold and it makes for a very lightweight knife. To get a handle that is stronger than one made of birch bark alone, I added other materials and put the birch bark in the middle. Then I increased the strength at the ends by adding sections of Sami knife leather and, at the very end, a section of horn. The result is a knife with all the advantages of birch bark, but with the strength of an all-wooden knife. See page 93 for a color photograph of this knife.

This knife is also fun to make. It is inspiring to be able to work with new materials. Naturally, it is just as easy to make it out of other materials, like layers of leather, or with small wooden inserts that offer a suitable contrast. To decorate the knife, I mounted a wooden plate on one side; you might want to engrave your initials on the plate. I wanted a finger guard that was not so large that the knife would not go down into an ordinary sheath. I also wanted the material used for the handle to be repeated in the sheath, so as to create a harmonious unit. (Like the previous knives, the sheath took longer to make than the knife.)

The choice of a blade was obvious from the beginning. I wanted a hand-forged, hand-laminated blade that was not too long. I began by filing the uneven knife tang straight, forming a conical narrowing toward the back. With a handle of such soft material, it is necessary to get a really tight fit between the material for the handle and the tang. Otherwise, there is a risk that some segment of the handle might come loose, and the play might cause damage that will eventually be impossible to fix.

Once the tang is filed, you will get a good fit between the tang and the upper horn piece. The handle is made in sections, which are then glued into place. First, glue the horn piece into place. Then allow it to dry for a day, while you prepare the other sections (Fig. 1).

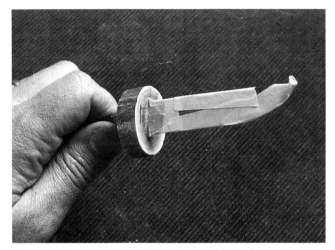

Fig. 1 *The upper piece of horn is glued into place.*

After the piece of horn comes a piece of Sami knife leather. Leather segments are cut out of the leather (Fig. 2), then glued together, one by one, with wood cement. Press them together by hand for a few minutes before clamping them (Fig. 3). This is to pre-

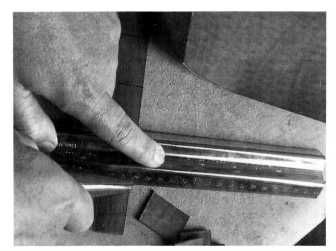

Fig. 2 *Cut the Sami knife leather.*

vent them from sliding apart. In the same manner, cut out the segments of birch bark for the middle section and glue them with wood cement. I try to use birch bark that is as thick and strong as possible to save labor, and because it is easier to work with. Finally, do the same with the back section of leather segments.

When all the sections have dried, it is time to begin to mount them. Make the holes for the tang in every one of them as accurately as possible. Then use epoxy to glue the sections in the proper order, allowing the work to dry for a day between each one (Fig. 4). Before riveting, it is important to see that every detail is in order, since you have so little time to make corrections before the glue hardens.

Rivet the handle behind the rear section of leather segments (Fig. 5). There will be a cap over the rivet, partly because the knife will look slimmer and more elegant, and partly because it prevents rust from coming into the knife through an exposed rivet.

After another day's drying time, the handle is ready to be roughly sawed. Trace the shape of the handle, using the pattern, then saw off the upper and lower pieces, then the sides (Fig. 6, page 129).

You have now reached the point at which the handle itself should be shaped (Figs. 7 and 8, page 129). In this case, do not use the rasp. It is too hard and, in the worst case, can tear loose some of the segments. Instead, use a knife and various files. Begin by shaping the finger guard and the area around it. Make good use of various round files. Your thumb is very useful in controlling the files. Protect your thumb by wrapping two or three layers of adhesive tape around it.

The corner of the handle is cut off with a knife, then the handle can be shaped. File the handle at an angle the whole time and apply gentle pressure. Continue using the file until the handle has its final shape.

After this is done, it is time to install the rear piece of horn. It saves a great deal of time to wait until this point to do this. The horn piece can then be made large enough to fit almost perfectly. This

Fig. 3 *The leather segments are glued and pressed.*

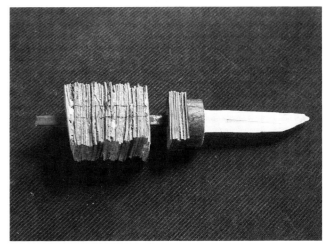

Fig. 4 *The middle section of the handle is glued.*

enables you to avoid filing off excess horn. Make an indentation for the rivet washer on the inside of the horn piece. Then drill holes for the screw that is screwed in through the horn piece and into the handle from the back.

When you have screwed the piece into place, you will be able to see how much horn sticks out beyond the handle. First, file it off. You should also put glue on the screw so that it attaches well to the handle. When the glue has hardened, you can give the rear horn piece its final shape. Begin sanding with sandpaper, going from very coarse paper to very fine paper (Fig. 9, page 130).

Before the surface treatment, make and fit the oval plate on the side of the handle. First, make the plate out of birch. The edges of the plate must lean inward somewhat so the plate presses tightly into the hollowed-out area. Then position it on the side of the handle and trace its outer contours. Make the hollow area in the birch bark section with a small knife and chisel. When you get a good fit between the plate and the indentation, glue the plate with wood cement and press it into place with a clamp. To protect the handle, a layer of leather is placed on each side while the knife is in the clamp.

When the plate has dried, the surface is sanded

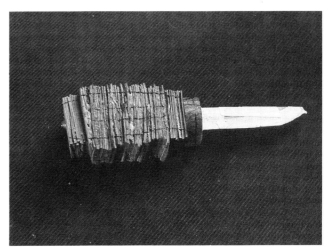

Fig. 5 *The handle is riveted and ready to be roughly sawed, according to the pattern.*

down so that it conforms to the handle. If you want, you can use a small knife to engrave the wood. Before you surface treat the knife with a pore closer and oil treatment, strengthen the engraved plate by applying a couple of protective layers of clear varnish (Fig. 10, page 130). It is better to do this now than to wait until after the oil treatment.

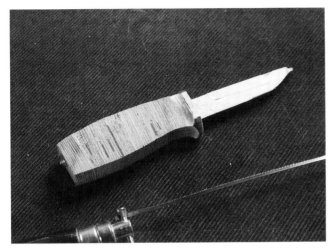

Fig. 6 *The handle, roughly sawed out*

Fig. 7 *The handle is shaped...*

THE SHEATH

Making the sheath is a more detailed process than making the knife, but is fun nonetheless. As usual, make the front and back sides of the sheath individually. Begin with the front side. It should be constructed from the same materials as the handle. The difference is that curly grained birch is used instead of horn. Birch is at the top, then comes a section of leather segments, a section of birch bark segments, a section of leather again, and, at the very bottom end, a section of curly grained birch. The leather sections are cut out in a suitable size (Fig. 11, page 131), then glued together with wood cement under pressure.

Cut the birch bark segments and glue them under pressure the same way you did with the leather segments. Then do the same with another leather section. (These three sections must be approximately the same width and length.) At the very bottom, saw out a piece of curly grained birch that will probably fit. The sections can't be glued to each other yet, because they would break apart while the hollowed-out area for the blade is being made. Instead, make the hollowed-out area in each section individually (Fig. 12, page 131).

It is practical to make a pattern of the sheath

Fig. 8 *...with files of various types.*

with a hollowed-out area for the blade in it. The loose sections are then held together by hand, while the space for the hollowed-out area is traced on the inside. Then the hollowed-out area is made in each section individually. Make sure that each part of the hollowed-out area is the same depth.

When you have a hollowed-out area that fits together well, glue all the sections together with wood cement. Everything is now allowed to dry thoroughly (Figs. 13 and 14, pages 131-32).

Next, make the back piece. Saw out a piece of

Fig. 9 *The sanded handle*

birch that is large enough for the entire back side. The plate is made broader at the top and bottom so that it will reach. By reversing the pattern, you can sketch the contours of the back piece. I use

lowed-out area, then chisel it out to a suitable depth (Fig. 15, page 132). The hollowed-out areas in the front and back pieces should match.

Before the front and back can be glued together, the contours of the sheath are sawed out of the back piece with a coping saw. Then the contact surfaces between the front and back should be sanded flat with a large piece of sandpaper attached to a board. There is no problem with the back piece, but be very careful with the front so as not to wear it down too far.

After you have checked that the surfaces fit flat against each other, glue them together with wood cement (Fig. 16, page 132) and clamp.

After drying, saw the outer contours of the front side cleanly, using the sawed-out back side as a model. The next step is to shape the broad sides of the sheath, the front side first. If you use really thick pieces to construct the front side, roughly saw out the correct profile. Otherwise, carefully work your way down with a rasp and file. The profile must be final in its shape before you go on. Work the back

Fig. 10 *The handle is decorated and ready for oiling.*

tracing/carbon paper to transfer the shape of the hol-lowed-out area for the blade to the back section. First, saw the upper edge of the sheath straight. Then use a large knife to cut out the contours for the hol-

side the same way.

Now make the outer contours of the sheath really tidy with a file. Continually measure and com-pare with the sheath pattern. This is quite a

130

time-consuming process, so don't give up before you reach your goal.

Then go back to the front side of the sheath and mark the center line of the sheath along its entire length. From there, shape each side, sloping toward the sides. Finally, there must be a ridge that goes along the entire length of the sheath (Fig. 17, page 133). Making the ridge is very time-consuming, because the material is so hard to work with. When you reach this point, drill the hole in the bone for the strap, drilling from both sides so that it is not crooked. Then shape the area around the hole and use a knife to shape the top of the lower sheath.

Once the whole front side is roughly cut out, it is easier to make the area toward the top of the lower sheath where the leather upper sheath will fit. Insert the finished knife into the sheath and sketch the outer contours against the top of the lower sheath. This tells you how broad and long to make the area where the leather upper sheath will grab hold. Space for the flange needs to be added at the very top of the lower sheath for the upper sheath to grab on to. Shaping the area for the upper sheath to grab on is probably the most time-consuming part of making the sheath. The upper sheath must fit the knife perfectly.

The area where the upper sheath will grab hold and the flange are cut and filed slowly. Use the knife to test several times before everything fits.

The front and back sides of the sheath must now be riveted together with wooden rivets. The rivets should be slightly conical, with a 3- to 4-mm (⅛- to ⁵⁄₃₂-inch) diameter, and made from a very hard type of wood. Drill a 3-mm (⅛-inch) hole into a very hard wood, and push the slightly conical rivets through this hole with the help of a piercer. Once

Fig. 12 *The hollowed-out area is cut into each section.*

Fig. 11 *The leather sections are cut out.*

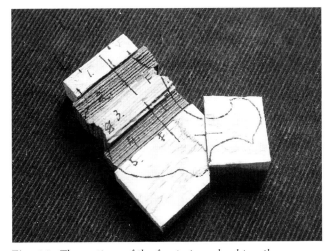
Fig. 13 *The sections of the front piece glued together*

131

Fig. 14 *The front piece from the inside*

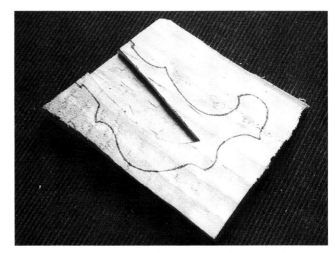

Fig. 15 *The back piece with the hollowed-out area for the knife blade is ready.*

the rivets are in the holes, they try to regain their original size and swell into place, hard and fast. Then you can use a knife to cut them down so that they are flush with the front side.

After all these steps, go over the entire sheath with a knife and file before the final sanding.

I choose Sami knife leather or shoe leather for the upper sheath, since both are very resistant to wear and tear. At the bottom of the upper sheath, add two small triple braids made of thin leather for decoration (see page 124 for instructions). These have to be added before the leather is softened, because the triple braids are glued to the inside through slots in the leather.

Before the leather upper sheath can be sewed, a layer of plastic wrap has to be wrapped around the knife handle to protect it. Then the indentation behind the finger guard is filled in with modeling clay so that the handle will be completely spool shaped. Otherwise, it will not be possible to remove the knife when the leather has dried.

An additional layer of plastic wrap is wrapped around the knife handle as protection against moisture and against the modeling clay. Put a couple of layers of paper between the layers of plastic wrap and above the modeling clay. Otherwise, the upper

sheath will become too tight. Then sew the upper sheath with a saddler's stitch, leaving an "ear" to attach the hanger (see page 62, Fig. 11 for instructions).

When the upper sheath has dried a few hours after sewing, decorate it. This is something that needs to be repeated several times during the next few hours so that the decorations will be permanent.

After a couple of days, when the upper sheath has completely dried, strengthen its attachment by screwing a couple of brass screws into the back side (Fig. 18) and drilling a horn button into the front side (Fig. 19).

What remains is to make the hanger with a triple braid (see page 124), which is also adjustable lengthwise. The hanger is attached to the "ear" on the back with a D-ring.

Then color the inside and all the visible edges of the upper sheath black. Rub beeswax into these surfaces, then polish them until completely shiny with a bone folder or something similar.

Give the leather the usual treatment: grease it with leather grease, which can be absorbed in several layers, then polish it with shoe cream to get it shiny. See Figs. 18 and 19 for the finished knife.

132

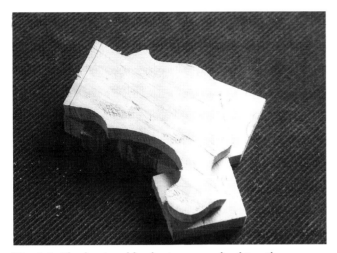

Fig. 16 *The front and back pieces are glued together.*

Fig. 18 *Back view of the finished sheath with the upper sheath and hanger in place*

Fig. 17 *The basic shape of the lower sheath has been made with a knife.*

Fig. 19 *A front view of the finished sheath*

133

THE OLD TIMER

The summer farm knife has very old roots, particularly in Dalarna, Sweden, where it was often carried by herder girls. The cap serves to prevent the knives from getting lost. As is the tradition, this knife has a curly grained birch handle and a laminated, hand-forged blade. The decorations on the sheath are my addition.

T his knife is known as a *cap knife* or *summer farm knife*. The sheath has a cap made of the same leather as the sheath itself, which slides on a leather strap that acts as the hanger. The cap is very effective in preventing you from losing the knife. This type of knife has ancient ancestors, but the strongest foothold seems to have been in the Siljan district and the surrounding areas. From there, it spread to neighboring parts of Sweden and was also found in Finland and other areas of Europe. See page 94 for a color photograph of this knife.

As far as selecting materials for the knife, I followed the tradition with a handle of curly grained birch, and a welded, laminated blade. On the other hand, I did not make the sheath of raw leather, but rather of vegetable-tanned leather, with or without a rough edge. Softer leather is better at holding the cup tightly over the knife. I am not completely loyal to the original in another respect—the old knives were often completely smooth or sparsely decorated, while I have decorated mine.

In respect to the shape of the handle, it is a good idea to stick to the original, straight type of handle without a curve at the back end, or finger guard at the front. Both the shape of the sheath and the cap limit excesses in handle design. However, certain other types of handles can also work well.

A few years ago, I made a cap knife with a conical handle and a finger guard on both the upper and lower sides, but it required a great deal of extra work to sew the sheath. I was forced to fill in all the indentations with modeling clay, so I could mold the shape as straight as possible before it was sewed. I sewed that sheath directly over the knife.

Make this knife in exactly the same manner as described on page 24. See Fig. 1.

Fig. 1 *The finished knife with a welded blade and handle of curly grained birch*

THE SHEATH

There are several ways of making a knife sheath with a cap. The top of the cap can be sewed with a seam that begins on the upper part of the front side and goes down toward the back side, or a horizontal plate can be sewed on the top side.

The sheath can be sewed over a last. Sew a ways over the last, then cut off the cap from the sheath when it has dried. Sewing over a last requires determining the exact shape of the piece of leather before fitting it around the last. This may mean a lot of failures before you succeed. To help yourself along the way, you can do two things.

Wrap the last with paper, then cut it out and you will get somewhat of a picture of how the leather piece should be cut. There is no problem with the paper around the last. It is harder to shape the paper around the cap; then it might be difficult to see which type of leather is needed there. But it can be done, and it is important not to give up.

The second method involves wrapping the last with masking tape, which is then cut up in the middle on the back side. I use this method often myself.

You should not expect to succeed the first time with either of these methods. Once you find exactly the right shape, make a pattern so that you can make

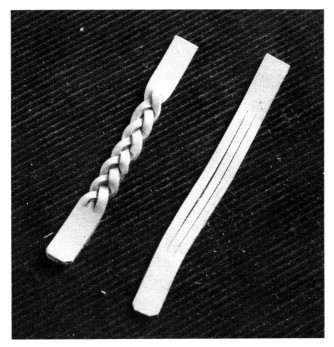
Fig. 2 *Making the braids*

Fig. 3 *The braids are colored with grain blacking.*

Fig. 4 *The handle is wrapped in plastic wrap.*

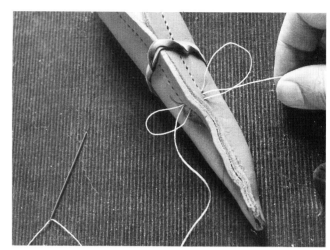

Fig. 6 *The lower part of the sheath is sewed.*

as many fine sheaths as you like. With a last, you can choose to sew the sheath and cap separately. Once they have dried, they can be joined so that they fit over the knife just right.

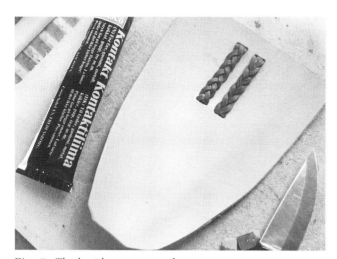

Fig. 5 *The braids are mounted.*

The disadvantage of using a last is that you always have to make knives that are exactly the same size. Otherwise, they won't fit in the sheath. So that I can free myself from this restriction and shape the knife the way I like, I use a third method: I use

the knife itself as a last and sew the sheath and cap around it. To simplify the process, you can sew a saddler's stitch through a piece of leather that is a little larger than what you'll need. Then you don't need to precut the exact shape, but simply trim down the edges after you're finished sewing. Using a last yields a sheath with a somewhat more elegant appearance, with seams that are less evident, but, to me, this is a small matter.

Begin by oiling the blade and wrapping it with masking tape so tightly that moisture can't penetrate. If you wrap the blade in at least a couple of layers, you will have a little space around the knife once the tape is removed and the sheath is completed.

I have placed two braided decorations on the front side of the sheath. Making these braids is the first step (Fig. 2, page 135). (The braids are common triple braids described on page 124.) I make them with a 9-mm-wide ($^{11}/_{32}$-inch) leather band of thin reindeer leather. When both braids are ready, dye them with grain blacking, in a color you choose at the beginning (Fig. 3, page 135). It can't be done later, partly because they are surrounded by naturally colored leather. The braids have to dry properly before they can be mounted. Sometimes I carefully wrap the knife handle in a few layers of plastic wrap as protection against wet leather (Fig. 4). The entire

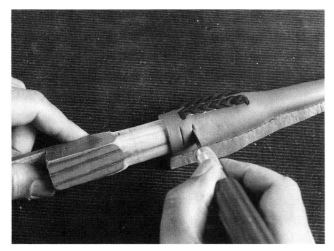

Fig. 7 *Cut the holes for the strap.*

Fig. 9 *Cut the leather for the cap.*

Fig. 8 *Round wedges are punched into the holes for the strap while the knife is in place.*

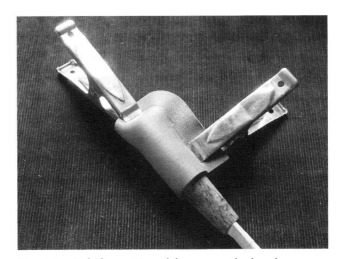

Fig. 10 *Mark the position of the seam with glue clamps.*

handle does not need to be protected, only the portion that is covered by the sheath.

Now it is time to measure the vertical center of the piece of leather to be cut out for the sheath. The braids will be mounted on each side of it and parallel to it (Fig. 5). With a very soft lead pencil, mark where the braids are to go. (The pencil marks can be erased afterwards.) Using a hollow punch and a chisel, make four rectangular holes where the braids will be inserted. Fold the braids down on the back

side and glue with contact adhesive (see Fig. 5).

When the glue has dried properly, put the leather piece in warm water for at least an hour. Then fold the leather around the handle and hold it together with several glue clamps that mark where the seam will go. Next, mark the distance between the stitches with a leather pricking iron, then poke the vertical holes with an awl. Sew the seam (Fig. 6).

Now make the holes on the sides of the sheath for the strap. Make two horizontal, parallel cuts a

137

few centimeters (¾ inch) apart with a chisel. The knife can't be in the sheath when you do this, or it will be damaged by the chisel. Instead, remove the knife from the sheath and replace it with a wooden dummy to hold up the sheath against the chisel (Fig. 7, page 137).

Stretch out the hole between the cuts with a rounded object, creating a channel or tunnel for the the strap (Fig. 8, page 137). The rounded objects can remain in place while you remove the wooden

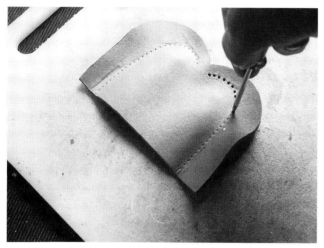

Fig. 11 *Make the hole for the seam with an awl.*

dummy and insert the knife in its place. Note that the stretched-out channels have to match the thickness of the strap that you intend to use. The sheath can now be left to dry, which takes at least a day.

For the cap, find a suitable piece of leather (Fig. 9, page 137). Finding the right shape for this piece may be a problem. I use the tested method of marking the position of the seam with glue clamps. The piece of leather is folded around the end of the handle with what will become the seam at the back. Allow the glue clamps to follow the shape of the handle all the way from the back and up over the top of the handle (Fig. 10, page 137). The clamps make an impression in the leather surface approximately where the seam needs to go.

If this method is hard to follow, you can always sew the seam directly. Simply clamp where the seam is to go with your fingers and sew from the top and toward the back. The leather must be completely wet before any sewing, or it will be impossible to sew. The seam can begin a ways down on the front side, or up at the top. See Figs. 11 and 12.

When the cap is sewn, cut out the hole for the strap. In order to avoid damaging the knife, pull the cap off of the knife and put it on a wooden last to cut against (Fig. 13). Make the horizontal cuts for

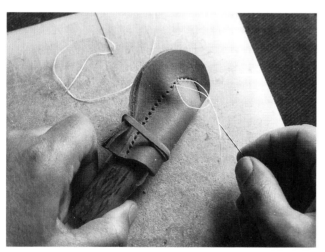

Fig. 12 *The seam is sewed.*

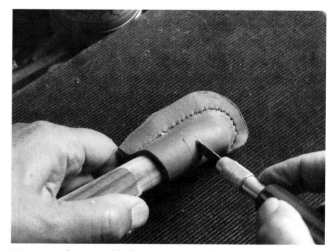

Fig. 13 *The tunnel holes are cut into the cap.*

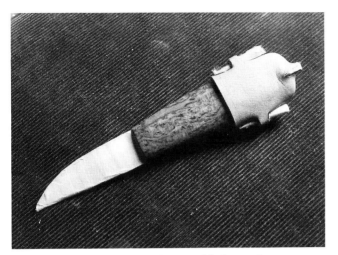

Fig. 14 *Sew the cap while the tunnel holes are being stretched out.*

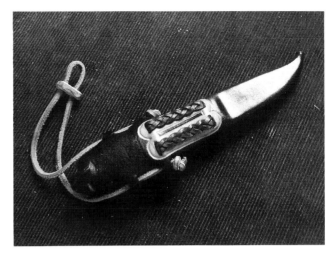

Fig. 16 *The finished sheath*

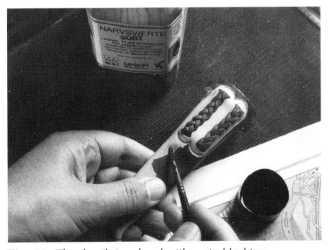

Fig. 15 *The sheath is colored with grain blacking.*

the hole with the same distance and at the same height on each side. It is often necessary to stretch out the tunnels where the strap will go in steps. You can begin with a narrow round object and progress to increasingly thicker ones (Fig. 14).

When the cap has dried, begin to fit it onto the sheath so that it will be completely tight, and at the proper height. (The cap should have been made with

proper measurements when it was sewed.) Now all the seams can be trimmed down to the proper height, using a knife. You can use an edge beveler to trim down the edges of the seam.

The sheath is now ready to be colored with a suitable shade of grain blacking (Fig. 15). Do this by painting at least three layers on the entire sheath so that it will be as well-covered as possible. Allow the grain blacking to dry thoroughly between coats. In addition, polish each new layer of blacking with a soft rag. If you made the sheath out of regular vegetable-tanned leather, you can stiffen it up by adding a couple of layers of clear varnish on the inside.

What remains is to cut a leather strap to the correct thickness and length. Then it is threaded through the tunnels and knotted as shown in Fig. 16. The entire sheath is greased with several layers of leather grease until the leather is saturated. Then the sheath is polished, and a layer of creamy shoe polish can be added to increase its shine.

HUNTING AND FISHING KNIFE

This is a multipurpose knife designed for hunting and fishing. The handle has Norwegian origins and is made from linden tree root, while the blade is rust-resistant and hand-forged. The sheath leather is vegetable-tanned, with a rough edge and an engraved decoration.

For this knife, you will need to make the sheath first, then make the knife to fit into it. This handle is made from a single piece of linden tree root. Refer to page 24 for instructions for an all-wood knife and to page 95 for a color photograph of this knife.

ENGRAVED SHEATH

In Sweden, it is still unusual to find an engraved knife sheath. Instead, we turn to Norway to find numerous examples of this method of decorating. It has been used there for a long time, particularly on sheaths that are used to hold woodcarving knives. In Norway, they have been used for decorative purposes and are worn with folk costumes. This type of sheath has certainly existed for hundreds, even thousands, of years as an almost indispensable tool—a companion in everyday life. Therefore, it is not unusual that we find some real masters of leather engraving in Norway. There are people who concentrate solely on this difficult art, and who only make sheaths. The variations in shape are endless, but the ornamentation on this sheath is based on Italian Acanthus Baroque from the 1500s, and depicts the acanthus plant. In the mid-1800s, this style made its entry as a sheath decoration in Norway, and is still used today.

A completely decorated sheath takes a considerable amount of time to make. The relatively limited experience I have with cutting leather decorations is not sufficient to teach all the tricks and fine details involved in the technique. Each knifemaker has his or her own individual method based on individual experience. I suggest you find a book devoted to leather decoration to use as a reference. Books on linoleum cutting or woodcarving may also be useful. Begin by practicing on scrap pieces.

Cutting a pattern into the dry sheath requires small but very sharp tools. The most common is a *V-iron* or *V-knife*, a small woodcarving tool with a V-shaped tip (Fig. 2). Other small woodcarving irons work relatively well, but the V-iron is the best, because the handle is so short that it is hidden inside your closed hand. Only the tip sticks out. Also, sometimes you can find a *goat's foot*, a carving tool used in Norway.

You can probably find a set of leatherworking tools at most craft stores. If you don't, you can buy an inexpensive set of small wood-engraving irons, which can be quite useful if they are properly sharpened and honed. A set of linoleum-cutting knives works even better. A set usually includes a short, wooden handle and several small, interchangeable blades. The sharpness of these tools can be improved if you harden the very tip by heating it

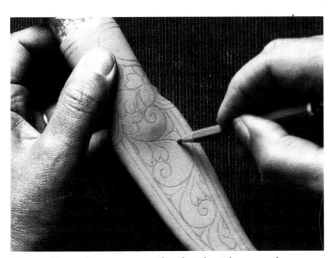

Fig. 1 *Draw the pattern on the sheath with a pencil.*

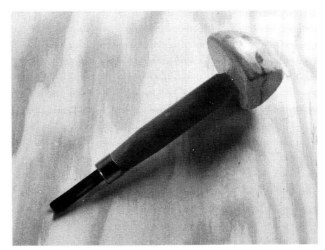

Fig. 2 *The V-iron or V-knife*

141

over a clean flame (225°–230° C or 373°–382° F) until it becomes yellowish-red. Then dip it in cold water at once. The tip becomes very hard, but also very brittle, so treat it carefully.

Finely hone and polish a fine edge on your carving tools. Experiment by sharpening the iron in various ways. Try a straight edge, a tip that sticks out, or a recessed tip, to find out which one works best for you. A pointy knife will also be a great help in your work. A scalpel with a pointy blade is sharp and useful. No matter which type of cutting tool you choose, ideally the the handle of the tool should be short enough to hide inside the palm of your hand.

THE TECHNIQUE

Let me first say that it is not particularly easy to carve out a beautiful (and balanced) decoration. But this should definitely not prevent you from becoming outstanding in this field someday. In order to help you avoid common mistakes, I will give you some advice based on my own experience.

The sheath to be decorated should be made of high-grade leather. It can be 3 to 4 mm (⅛ to ⁵⁄₃₂ inch) thick if you want a margin left over after cutting and

Fig. 3 *Hold the knife like this while cutting.*

still have a strong sheath. It is also important that the leather surface be as smooth and flat as possible. The soft, thin, and slightly flimsy leather from the belly and throat of an animal will not work; it will be like cutting into dough. Try to find some insole leather, which is ideal for engraving.

The first step will be to sketch your pattern on the sheath. I usually sketch it on greaseproof paper. Moisten the leather's surface a little, add some plastic wrap (or something similar), and, on top of that, place the greaseproof paper. It is easy to transfer the pattern by tracing it. When the surface of the sheath has dried, trace over the lines with a soft pencil or a knitting needle (Fig. 1, page 141).

Carving requires a great deal of concentration—especially as the iron is moving through the leather surface. Despite what you might imagine, it is a concerted movement of the entire upper body—not just the hand and fingers—that is needed. The strength that moves the iron forward has to come from your upper body, back, and shoulders. Therefore, find a comfortable working position that won't tire you out.

I prefer to work at a north window because of the soft, even light. If you don't have access to a north window, you can compensate by covering the entire window with a thin curtain or other translucent material, so the window provides diffuse light that makes it easy to see what you are cutting—as well as the results.

If you aren't satisfied with the handle on the V-knife, you can make a new one to fit your hand. The knife must be like a part of your hand, nearly like a sixth finger. With a homemade knife, it will be easier to follow an exact sketch, so the knife can nearly go parallel to the surface of the sheath. Hold the knife securely between your thumb and fingers. The thumb almost rests against the tip of the V-iron; the fingertips around the handle can angle the knife in slightly different directions (Fig. 3). The knife is placed against the leather surface, controlled with the thumb and the fingers, and pushed forward, using gentle pressure from the palm of the hand.

142

The angle between the knife and the leather is important. A knife held at too severe of an angle carves too deeply into the leather surface and can get stuck. If it is held at too shallow of an angle, the knife slips off the leather and you must cut again. Practice getting the right angle on all the scrap pieces of leather you can spare.

While cutting, always keep your thumb in contact with the leather surface; otherwise, you will lose control of your tool. Put the knife at a right angle, keep your thumb still, and let the palm of your hand push out the tip of the knife past the thumb as far down as you can reach (about ½ to 1 cm or ¼ to ⅜ inch). For short cuts, hold your thumb still. If you hold the work piece still, you will get a straight cut. If you twist the work piece at the same time that you push the knife forward, you will get a curved cut of the same length.

With practice, you can make longer straight and curved cuts if you let your thumb gently slide along the leather surface with a forward movement. For short cuts, hold the thumb still against the leather surface. For long cuts, slide the thumb gently toward the leather surface and follow with the knife. To make a curved cut, it is better to twist the work piece than to twist your hand and arm. I usually support the work piece on top of a small, thick book covered with a rag. Then it is much easier to move the work piece than if you place it directly on the surface of the table. You can certainly use something other than a book, as long as the piece you are working on can easily be turned sideways.

Of course, the depth and width of the cut depends on how large a V-iron you are using, but the angle of the iron against the leather surface is just as important. A large angle gives a deep and wide cut, and a small angle gives a narrow and shallow cut. There is a maximum depth to which the iron can reach before it sticks. You will soon learn where the limits are.

If you want to make a cut that is just as deep as it is thick, you must continually reduce the angle as the cut is made. If you don't reduce the angle, the tip will cut down into the leather again. The technique requires a good deal of practice to get a clean cut, but don't give up! When you have learned it, the memory will rest in your hand. The width and depth of the cut varies simply by raising or lowering your hand. But don't make any sudden movements upward or downward. The slightest change causes an immediate deflection. If your hand moves vertically, you will get an uneven cut.

For finer cuts, you will need a smaller iron to get deep enough. Cuts that are increasingly narrow are made by gradually lowering the hand toward the end of the cut. If you managed to get an evenly thick cut that is wider or narrower in one direction, you can simply turn the sheath and cut from the other side at the same depth.

When you make curved cuts and twist the work under the tip of the V-iron, only experience can tell you how quickly you need to turn and how high you need to hold the knife. If the outer sides of the curve are too deep and get frayed edges, then apply a little more pressure on the iron toward the opposite side. Try to begin with the innermost curves first, and work your way out. For example, when you make a cut that is perpendicular to one you already made, make sure that the "stomach" of the knife doesn't go in and disturb the previous cut. If you are considering filling a surface with a pattern of diamond-shaped cuts, then do not make the angle between the cuts too small.

One of the most common beginner mistakes is cutting too deeply. Caution and concentration help somewhat. It is better to cut too little than too much. Later, when you are more confident, this won't be a problem. Ultimately, everything depends on how much you practice.

Follow this sequence when you carve your designs:

1. Make the frame cuts first (Fig. 4).
2. There are probably surfaces inside your figures that need to be sunken, or places where

your figures may need to stand out better. Cut out and remove these with a potato peeler or a small hobby knife (Fig. 5).

3. Finally, use a small V-iron to cut the fine details, such as the veins in the leaves (Fig. 6).

SURFACE TREATMENT

When the engraving is finished, the surface needs an after-treatment. First, sand it with the finest sandpaper you can get. You can singe off the loose leather strips with a flame or blowtorch that rapidly sweeps over the leather surface. Avoid candles and matches—they mainly blacken the leather.

If you want to keep the leather's own color, grease the sheath with leather grease or with a thinned varnish (clear lacquer or knotting varnish). Knotting varnish should be thinned out with methylated spirits. Apply several layers, and allow drying in between.

If you want the sheath to be a brown color, color it with brown grain blacking (Fig. 7). Then apply several layers of the varnish solution described above. If you want it completely black, then use equal parts of black grain blacking and varnish as a final treatment on top of the black sheath.

Fig. 4 *Cut out the outer contours of the design.*

Fig. 5 *Cut out the areas between the flowers.*

Collect books, newspapers, articles, and pictures of carved sheaths for inspiration. By studying them in detail, you can learn a great deal. Fig. 8 shows the finished sheath.

SHARPENING TOOLS

Leather cutting tools that are used frequently need to be sharpened and honed regularly. Dull tools only damage the leather surface, which is impossible to repair. The movements of the dull tool become hard to control. A properly sharpened tool usually only needs a light honing on a black Arkansas stone or some equivalent.

You should only grind when the bevel of the tool has a convex, rounded form, or if a tip or edge piece has broken off. This rough grinding is done on a grindstone. The grindstone should rotate against the edge. When you have ground an entirely flat surface (check against obliquely falling light), it is time to hone off the raw edge that has formed.

Begin honing on a rougher hone, like a medium-coarse Arkansas hone, then move on to the fine white or extra-fine black hone. Hold the tool in one hand so that the back edge of the bevel lies against the stone and the tip points slightly up into the air. Then sink the bevel downward so that it completely

Fig. 6 *Cut out the veins of the leaves.*

Fig. 7 *The knife sheath is colored with grain blacking.*

rests against the lower surface. Hold the tool diagonally in the forward and backward sanding motions.

It is easier to keep the bevel in the right position. Hold the fingertips of the other hand as straight over the bevel as possible. Then put a little pressure on the bevel. A lot of pressure is not necessary. Move the tool back and forth across the stone. Move consistently to another area of the stone to avoid hollowing out any one area. Move very quickly and rhythmically back and forth. Follow with your entire upper body. The proper angle is maintained by holding the arm immobile the entire time. When you leave the medium-coarse hone, hone off the scratches and raw edges with a white or black Arkansas hone.

You can check to see if you have succeeded by test cutting a small scrap piece of leather. If the tip "bites" immediately, it is ready to use. The older method of testing the edge against your thumbnail is also effective.

Fig. 8 *The finished knife sheath*

PREHISTORIC KNIFE

This knife design dates back to the Stone Age. The shape is for skinning, though early examples of this knife were made with blades of bone instead of steel. Used properly, this knife is very effective for skinning and is relatively easy to make. Because of its shape, the blade is equipped with an edge protector.

W hen excavating a Stone Age settlement in upper Lapland, archaeologists discovered a skinning knife that may have been used 6,000 years ago. The original knife was made of bone. In spite of that, it was excellent for skinning animals. The shape of the knife was very interesting, and so was the way it was used. It does not resemble any of the skinning knives we use today. In the original, the upright handle was wrapped with leather straps that were probably made from elk.

I decided to make a copy of the knife, using modern materials. The blade would be metal. The handle would be more refined than the original, but equally effective. I made a full-scale sketch of the blade, and sent it to one of the best knifesmiths to see if he would make it. It turned out very well. Once he got started, he made me several (Fig. 1). Refer to the color photograph of this knife on page 96.

In order to get the best possible sharpness and the greatest honing ability, the smith laminated the blade; it has a core of hardened steel surrounded by softer iron plates, which are forged together. The edge has both great hardness and high carbon content, while the iron supports the hard edge steel.

Of course, the blades could also be forged completely in steel. To my knowledge, they cannot be purchased anywhere, so, if you want one of these knives, you will need to order the blade from a smith. As can be seen from the photographs on this page, the blade's edge curve is slightly unusual. It is relatively straight on the bottom then forms a curve with a small radius. The curved part itself needs to look approximately like modern skinning knives. The blade is about 4 mm (5/32 inch) thick.

For the handle, I chose curly grained birch, which is hard, strong, and beautiful. The handle is shaped to be as comfortable as possible. You can try several different shapes, as long as the knife is easy and effective to use. There is a curved plate at the top of the handle, shaped according to the thumb. It

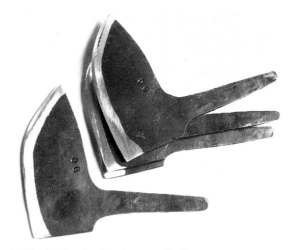

Fig. 1 *The blades for the skinning knife*

Fig. 2 *Shape the end of the handle.*

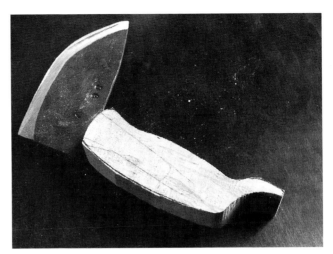

Fig. 4 *The shape of the handle is sawed out.*

Fig. 3 *The blade is attached to the handle.*

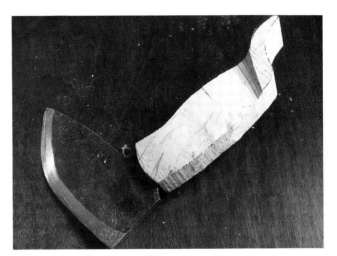

Fig. 5 *The sides are sawed out.*

has the important function of supporting the thumb when the edge of the knife is pressed against the skin in backward arching movements, which are constantly repeated. When the blade is well sharpened and honed, no great strength is needed to effectively skin an animal.

When you make a skinning knife like this, always use a cardboard pattern. It makes the job easier. Select a handle material that has sufficient dimensions. It is always good to have a little extra material to use in case something goes wrong. The edge of the handle that will be attached to the

blade is slightly arched. Shape it before you attach the blade.

Next, sketch the shape of the tang on the sides of the material for the handle. Then drill two holes in the end of the handle that touch the lines that have been drawn on the sides. Saw off the wood that remains between the holes, using a small compass saw. Then file the hole a little so that the tang fits into it with only a few centimeters (¾ inch) to spare. It is usually possible to pound the tang the last bit of the way into the handle.

Before you glue the tang in place, make sure the

147

upper end of the handle is shaped correctly (Fig. 2, page 147). Next, mix a small batch of epoxy glue—enough to coat the hole on the inside and the knife tang. Then fasten the blade with a vise, using pieces of wood on the sides as protection. Pound the tang

Fig. 6 *The final shape of the handle is made with a knife.*

into place with a rubber mallet. Allow the knife to rest for a few days until the glue has hardened properly (Fig. 3, page 147).

Then begin to shape the handle. At this point, the pattern comes in really handy. Trace the shape of the handle on the sides of the material. Begin with the upper and lower sides of the handle. These can be sawed out with a small coping saw (Fig. 4, page 147). When this is done, saw the sides (Fig. 5, page 147) and give them their final shape with a rasp and file.

It is quite easy to give the sides of the handle their shape. The shape must be increasingly narrow toward the end to provide the best grip. When the handle begins to have a really square shape, the job of rounding begins. Always do the first rough cutting of the edges with a knife so that you can have complete control over the work (Fig. 6).

At this point, there are two ways to make the final shape. Either leave the handle a little roughly cut, so that you can feel the surface of the wood, or finely sand the handle and give it a surface that is as

Fig. 7 *The finished knife*

fine as that of a regular knife. No matter which method you choose, follow the detailed instructions for making an all-wood handle on page 24. Refer also to the section on finishing techniques, page 32. Fig. 7 shows the finished knife.

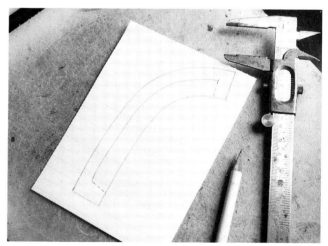

Fig. 8 *The shape of the sheath is traced on the leather material.*

Fig. 9 *Cut out the pieces for the sheath.*

THE SHEATH

Make the sheath out of either vegetable-tanned leather or shoe leather, so that it will be sturdy and strong.

This sheath consists of two side pieces of leather. Between them, another piece is permanently attached flush to the outer edge. In order to achieve the correct outer and inner shapes, trace the edge of the knife along the entire length of the leather. From there, it is easy to see what shape the sides and inner piece should have. Retrace the pattern on the leather with a darker pencil, then cut the shapes out (Figs. 8 and 9).

The next step is to glue the inner piece onto one of the side pieces (Fig. 10). These pieces must lie edge to edge against each other. At the very back of the sheath, a stop piece is also glued, which will prevent the knife from sliding out of the finished sheath (Fig. 11).

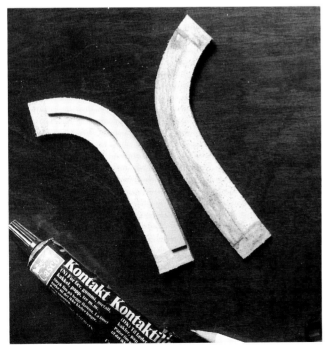

Fig. 10 *Glue in place the in-between layer.*

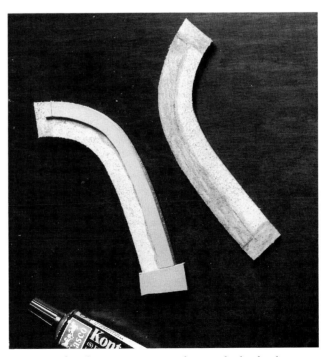

Fig. 11 *Glue the stop piece into place at the back edge.*

149

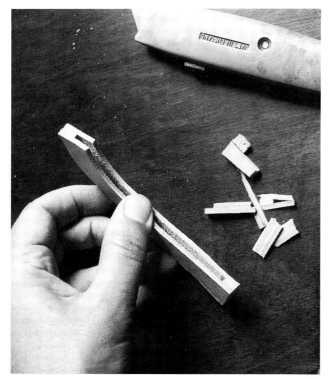

Fig. 12 *The sheath halves are glued together and cut cleanly.*

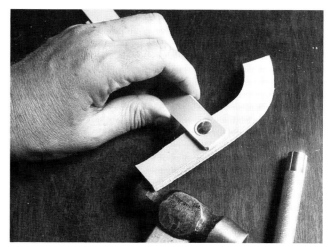

Fig. 13 *Riveting the strap.*

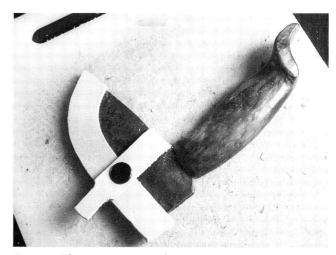

Fig. 14 *The snap is mounted.*

When these steps are complete, the other half is glued permanently to the pieces in the middle. At each step, make sure that everything is edge to edge. When the sheath has dried, it is a good idea to clean-cut the edges so that the sheath will become completely symmetrical (Fig. 12).

A strap that crosses over the blade exactly in front of the handle is necessary to keep the sheath in place. One end of the strap can be riveted on one side of the sheath (Fig. 13). On the opposite side, a strong snap is mounted so the strap can be attached to it (Fig. 14).

Having attached the snap, the simple sheath is almost finished. Only the surface treatment remains. The sheath can be dyed with grain blacking in the color of your choice (Fig. 15), greased with several layers of leather grease, then polished with cream shoe polish.

Fig. 15 *Dyeing the sheath*

INDEX

A NOTE ABOUT SUPPLIERS

Usually, the supplies you need for making the projects in Lark books can be found at your local craft supply store, discount mart, home improvement center, or retail shop relevant to the topic of the book. Occasionally, however, you may need to buy materials or tools from specialty suppliers. In order to provide you with the most up-to-date information, we have created a listing of suppliers on our Website, which we update on a regular basis. Visit us at www.larkbooks.com, click on "Craft Supply Sources," and then click on the relevant topic. You will find numerous companies listed with their web address and/or mailing address and phone number.